Two on the Aisle,
Three in a Van

Mary Lynn Dobson

A SAMUEL FRENCH ACTING EDITION

SAMUEL FRENCH

FOUNDED 1830

SAMUELFRENCH.COM
SAMUELFRENCH-LONDON.CO.UK

ISBN 978-0-573-70102-3

www.SamuelFrench.com
www.SamuelFrench-London.co.uk

FOR PRODUCTION ENQUIRIES

UNITED STATES AND CANADA
Info@SamuelFrench.com
1-866-598-8449

UNITED KINGDOM AND EUROPE
Theatre@SamuelFrench-London.co.uk
020-7255-4302

Each title is subject to availability from Samuel French, depending upon country of performance. Please be aware that *TWO ON THE AISLE, THREE IN A VAN* may not be licensed by Samuel French in your territory. Professional and amateur producers should contact the nearest Samuel French office or licensing partner to verify availability.

MUSIC USE NOTE

Licensees are solely responsible for obtaining formal written permission from copyright owners to use copyrighted music in the performance of this play and are strongly cautioned to do so. If no such permission is obtained by the licensee, then the licensee must use only original music that the licensee owns and controls. Licensees are solely responsible and liable for all music clearances and shall indemnify the copyright owners of the play(s) and their licensing agent, Samuel French, against any costs, expenses, losses and liabilities arising from the use of music by licensees. Please contact the appropriate music licensing authority in your territory for the rights to any incidental music.

IMPORTANT BILLING AND CREDIT REQUIREMENTS

If you have obtained performance rights to this title, please refer to your licensing agreement for important billing and credit requirements.

TWO ON THE AISLE, THREE IN A VAN was performed in the FringeNYC Festival, August 16th–29th, 2009, at the Connelly Theatre, New York. It was produced by Peter Riga Jr., Dan Whitten, and Tiger Theatricals. The production was directed by Mary Lynn Dobson with costumes by James Herrera and Sue Takacs, lighting by Tom Rowe. The production stage manager was Bob Dumpert. The cast was as follows:

VONDO	Gordon Joseph Weiss
JEANNIE	Letitia D. Townes
JEFF	Paul De Pasquale
MIKE	Jim Stanek
HARRIET	Terri Sturtevant
ERIC	Jonathan Wierzbicki *(certain performances)*
	John P. Dowgin *(certain performances)*
MEREDITH	Natascia Diaz
DANIEL	Stephen Medvidick
ROBIN	Madeline Blue
SCOTT	Rick Delaney

TWO ON THE AISLE, THREE IN A VAN was a winner and was performed as part of the Northern Kentucky University's YES Festival. The production was directed by Michael King.

CHARACTERS

MIKE – Director/stage manager, soon to be artistic director, good looking, genuinely nice, mid thirites.

JEANNIE – Stage manager, wardrobe person, techie in general, has grown to hate the actors, mid thirties to fifties.

VONDO – Techie, sometime actor, one time pot head, dressed as he was in high school–probably even in the same shirt, owner of the van, late fifties to sixties.

JEFF – The artistic director, forever trying to avoid disaster, high blood pressure and forever trying to avoid a stroke, fifties to early sixties.

SCOTT – The new guy from the Midwest, costume designer, wardrobe person, nice guy, thirties to late forties.

ERIC – Director, writer, actor, threatens greatness but delivers nonsense, constantly morbid, mid-thirties.

MEREDITH – Actress, usually gets the leads, a diva-wanna-be, feigns confidence, basically plain, mid-thirties.

DANIEL – Actor, idiot, thinks he's the ultimate theater persona, obsessed with dancing, mid to late twenties.

ROBIN – Actress, plays all the ingénue roles, you just want to hug her because she's cute as cute can be, innocent, naive, fifteen.

HARRIET – Actress, sometime wardrobe person, quick-witted, real, early sixties to seventies.

Note: Additional character descriptions can be found at the back of the script.

TIME

TWO ON THE AISLE, THREE IN A VAN takes place over a three and a half month span on a one unit set.

MANDATORY PLAYWRIGHT'S NOTE

By acquiring the rights to perform this play you are agreeing to abide by the conditions of the playwright's notes at the back of the script. They state certain specifics about the play that cannot be changed. It is mandatory that the director and actors read these notes before rehearsing and performing this play.

ACT I

Scene I

(Time: the present. At curtain, Deep Purple's "Smoke on the Water"* is played on an electric guitar. Only the introduction of the song is played. The scene is a parking lot in back of a theatre. A well-traveled van, which is at least 15 to 20 years old, is positioned so it is "parked" so the back is facing the audience. Its two back doors are open. The building has one commercial steel door, solid —no glass. There is a used-looking cooler next to the van. Sets from the show are being kept outside due to lack of wing space. There are racks with appropriate costumes hanging on them with a small tarp or cover on half the rack, which can be used to hide the costumes which will be seen in the upcoming scenes. There is a marquee stage left. It reads: "The Neighborhood Actors Summerfun Repertory Theatre – Now Playing – Hello Dolly". It's intermission of the first performance. [Note: throughout the play, the tech people should always be working on something for the next show opening.] **VONDO** *is sitting on the back of the van playing his electric guitar, at a medium-low volume, through a small amp next to where he sits. He's dressed exactly as he was in high school, jeans, sneakers and a tee shirt. His hair is semi-long or in a ponytail.* **JEANNIE** *lies in the van next to him – we only see her knees, hanging over the back edge of the van. She is dressed in jeans/shorts and a show-tee shirt or in "tech black".* **JEFF**, *the artistic director, enters from the theatre. It is obvious he has high blood pressure.*

---

*See Music Use Note on pg. 3.

JEFF. *(pissed)* VONDO! Have you seen Eric?

VONDO. No.

JEFF. If you do, tell him I'm going to kill him. You got that Vondo? Tell the man he's going to die.

VONDO. Okay, Boss.

> *(**JEFF** begins to exit, **MIKE** enters. **MIKE**'s a good-looking guy in jeans and a tee shirt. He carries an approximately 4x3 frame, no glass, for what will be a "stained glass window" for the next show.)*

JEFF. *(crosses to **MIKE**)* MIKE! Have you seen Eric?

MIKE. No.

JEFF. If you do, tell him I'm going to kill him. You got that Mike? Tell the man he's going to die.

MIKE. Okay.

JEFF. *(turns to **JEANNIE**)* JEANNIE!

JEANNIE. *(not sitting up)* I'll tell him!

> *(**JEFF** exits into the theatre, storming past **HARRIET** as she enters. She's in the chorus and is dressed in turn of the century garb. She looks at **MIKE** and shakes her head. **MIKE** crosses to the van where he, **JEANNIE** and **VONDO** eventually begin to work on the "church window" by taping either colored construction paper or colored cellophane into the empty panes of the window. Whatever materials are used should not be noisy, so as to not distract from the scene.)*

MIKE. *(to **HARRIET**)* Well, he told Eric to close Act I with a bang.

HARRIET. Yes he did. Oh, it's nice out here tonight. You know, I think I like being out here better than in the chorus room. I used to think you all were pretty silly not wanting to stay in the air-conditioning. But it's really quite pleasant out here.

MIKE. And more peaceful.

HARRIET. Well dear, anywhere away from Meredith is more peaceful. She's in there right now barking at Scott because, of all things, her gloves don't fit right. *(crosses to cooler)*

JEANNIE. *(sits up)* It's not about the gloves. She's just pissed because Robin's stealing the show.

HARRIET. I don't know about her. *(Takes a beer our of the cooler. Looks at her beer.)* Rheingold?* Who bought this?

VONDO. I did. I got it for you. I thought you might like it. I mean, you know, it's from your era.

HARRIET. So is polio, dear. Have you ever tasted this stuff?

VONDO. No. And I never will. I've given it up for life.

HARRIET. *(sweetly)* Yes well, thank you for the thought, honey. Perhaps tomorrow night during intermission I'll come out and churn some butter for everyone. *(puts beer back in cooler)*

JEANNIE. Hey Harriet, I thought you were you supposed to play Dolly. What happened?

HARRIET. Well…let's just say I graciously backed out when they switched directors.

(ERIC and MEREDITH enter. ERIC is a director/actor who would explore the dark side of Winnie the Pooh. He wears head to toe black. MEREDITH is the company's star who's on the neurotic side. She wears a Hello Dolly red sequined dress with red feathers in her hair.)

ERIC. I didn't feel you at all! You're not coming across to the audience. Continue like this and you'll ruin my play! Now tell me! Who is Dolly Levy?

MEREDITH. *(she rattles this off because she's said it a thousand times)* She's a widow cheated by death at the height of her sexuality. She rages against the bondage forced by the fraternal tyranny of a misogynistic world.

ERIC. Good. What else?

MEREDITH. She's a survivor. But, she wants to control the lives of those around her.

ERIC. Right!

---

* If Rheingold is unavailable, Schaefer or Ballantine may be substituted.

MEREDITH. And that's why she's a matchmaker.

ERIC. NO! I told you never to use that word! You're an actor, Meredith! See beyond the words! Dolly Levy sells and buys women for a fee. FOR A FEE! Dolly Levy is a pimp.

JEANNIE. *(to* **HARRIET***)* Dolly Levy's a pimp?

ERIC. *(to* **MEREDITH***)* Just because a playwright says something – doesn't mean they really mean it. They just give you clues.

VONDO. *(to* **HARRIET***)* Does this mean Carol Channing was a pimp?

ERIC. *(to* **MEREDITH***)* It's your job to "see beyond the words"!

JEANNIE. No, I can't see Carol Channing as a pimp.

MIKE. Me either. A muppet, maybe, but not a pimp.

VONDO. A Carol Channing muppet would be cute. She could have big, ping-pong ball eyes that go blinky, blinky, blinky.

MEREDITH. *(to* **VONDO***)* Stop! You're breaking my concentration. *(to* **ERIC***)* I can't act with this.

MIKE. Hey lighten up, guys.

ERIC. Peasant! This is a painful process. Meredith delves into parts of herself that she didn't even know existed to create her character.

MEREDITH. *(to* **JEANNIE***)* I suffer for my performance.

JEANNIE. So does everyone who sees it.

MEREDITH. *(to* **ERIC***)* I can't act with this. (**MEREDITH** *walks behind the van.)*

*(**DANIEL** enters. He's playing a waiter and wears a white shirt, black bow tie, red vest, black pants and spats.)*

DANIEL. Eric! Eric! Eric! I just got this idea. It's so entertaining! Instead of me just pointing up the stairs and saying, *(blandly)* "Rudy, she's here." How about I play the waiter who will not bow to the Gestapo tactics of the maitre d'? I can do a strength move. Watch – *(runs to one end of the stage)* Rudy, *(runs to* **ERIC**, *does a spin, lands on one knee and points with a big gesture)* SHE'S HERE!

ERIC. Do it the way we rehearsed it.

DANIEL. How about we use it in the kick line…

ERIC. Not now, Daniel!

(exits after **MEREDITH** *behind van)*

JEANNIE. Hey Daniel, they said at least six weeks to fix my coffee maker. I loved that coffee maker. It was the only good thing that came out of my marriage.

DANIEL. I'm sorry already. It was an accident, okay?

JEANNIE. Accident or not, you're buying me coffee every day till I get it back.

DANIEL. Okay! God! *(exasperated, exits)*

HARRIET. Well, I'm going to check my make-up.

VONDO. Remember Harriet, cast party at my place tonight.

HARRIET. Yes, I'll be there. *(to* **MIKE***)* Oh boy, Rheingold for everyone.

*(***ROBIN ROSENBLATT*** enters. She's 15 and is playing Minnie Fay and wears a ruffley Victorian dress with a big bow in her hair.)*

HARRIET. Oh your song sounded great, Robin. *(exits)*

ROBIN. *(upset)* I'm not Robin. Mike, do you think Jeff'll get mad if I ask him to change the program when he prints more for next week?

MIKE. Why, what's the matter?

ROBIN. He put the wrong name in. *(shows him the program)* I wanted a stage name, so me and my friends made up one. But Jeff forgot and printed Robin Rosenblatt.

MIKE. Who are you this show?

ROBIN. Tapestry Meadowlark.

*(***MIKE***,* **JEANNIE** *and* **VONDO** *try to suppress their smiles.)*

ROBIN. *(seeing their reactions)* You don't think it's good? I can change it. What should I change it to?

VONDO. Sydney Australia?

JEANNIE. Summers Eve?

ROBIN. *(to* **MIKE** *with a big smile)* Summers Eve? I like that!

MIKE. *(looks at* **JEANNIE***)* Let's just leave it like it is, okay? I'll take care of it.

ROBIN. *(big smile)* Thanks, Mike! You're so nice! *(hugs him and exits)*

ERIC. *(enters, calling back to* **MEREDITH***)* That's better, you almost have it. Just give me a little more *Super Fly*. God, I can't believe the crap I have to put up with on this show. Things will be different when I do *Medea*.

VONDO. Oh, it *is Medea*. I thought they just spelled media wrong. What's it about?

ERIC. You don't know what *Medea's* about? Blatant ignorance!

MIKE. It's your basic Greek tragedy. Woman scorned, kills lover's wife, kills her children, kills lover's children, kill's lover's wife's father, escapes by chariot that flies through sky. *(to* **ERIC***)* So which version are you doing, Euripides or Anouilh?

ERIC. Oh, please! I'm doing *my* version. As Associate Artistic Director, it is my *job* to see that new works find their way to our stage. Michael, you're somewhat a music connoisseur, are you not?

MIKE. Yeah?

ERIC. Perhaps you can help me find the perfect music for the pinnacle of Act I. Medea's murder of her children. I was thinking of using the theme from Psycho, but I thought that was, you know, a little too typical.

JEANNIE. Besides, aren't you saving that for your wedding song?

ERIC. *(to* **JEANNIE***)* Simple maid, your life is so sad. *(to* **MIKE***)* I need something with a beat – to coincide with Medea stabbing them.

MIKE. I'll see what I can come up with.

ERIC. I've told Scott to line the costumes with blood packs. That way, when they're stabbed, my actors will bleed like stuck pigs.

MIKE. You do realize that in all Greek tragedies the violence happens off-stage.

ERIC. Well, guess what Toto, we're not in Greece anymore. And I'm not just planning murder, I'm planning dismemberment as well. Behind the murder scene I'm flashing slides of pigs led to slaughter, tanks closing in on Tiananmen Square, the ambush scene from Bonnie and Clyde! *Guts* oozing out of the actors and spilling into the polka-dotted laps of the blue hairs in the front row! Yes! *(smiles and exits)*

JEANNIE. Something tells me his mother breast-fed him just a little too long.

MIKE. Know where he gets these brilliant ideas for his adaptations of great novels? Cliff Notes. He won't read the novel, cause he says reading the book just gives you the author's side of the story. You know what he had the nerve to say to me today? That I'm intellectually inferior to him. *(shakes his head and smiles)* I love it.

I've got my Master's in literature and I'm getting dissed by the manager of a Dairy Queen. *(speaking as* **ERIC***)* You people are all fools! I have such insight of the world that even I fear my own mind. I am astute! I am superior! I am intellectually above you all! *(holds arm out, handing someone an ice cream cone)* Do you want sprinkles with that?

*(***SCOTT*** enters completely panicked, with a clipboard with a pencil attached by a sting and long, white evening gloves. He's the costume designer and is dressed conservatively. Shorts and a button down short-sleeve shirt.)*

SCOTT. Get ready for fireworks.

JEFF. *(enters in a panic, holding red gels.)* VONDO!

*(***JEFF*** deliberately speaks into ***VONDO***'s face.)*

I want you to hide these. Put them somewhere and under no circumstances give them to Eric. You got that, Vondo? Keep these away from Eric.

ERIC. *(offstage)* WHERE ARE MY GELS?

JEFF. *(hands* **VONDO** *the gels)* SIT ON THEM! EAT THEM! HIDE THEM NOW!

ERIC. *(enters)* WHO TOOK MY GELS?!

JEFF. YOU! YOU ARE GOING TO DIE! I AM GOING TO KILL YOU! YOU GOT THAT ERIC? I AM GOING TO KILL YOU DEAD! I can't believe you had the girls in the parade number strip down to their corsets! And as if that weren't bad enough, ya had the cotton candy vendor soliciting sex! WHAT IS WRONG WITH YOU?

ERIC. *(calmly)* Each one of these women is desperate for a man and they use Dolly as their pimp. They're hookers. It's dark. It's perverse. It's real.

JEFF. *(stares at him)* IT'S *HELLO DOLLY!* How did you get like this? Did your parents like, lock you in a box until you were twelve? Was your only friend the vacuum cleaner? What is it? I'd really like to know.

ERIC. I am breathing new life into stale, musical sewage! Why can you not appreciate the important work I do at this theatre?

JEFF. The only reason you do *any* work at this theatre is because your goddamn aunt owns the goddamn building!

ERIC. And might I remind you if it weren't for me getting Aunt Phyllis involved here, this place would have shut down six years ago.

JEFF. You don't have to. She does every time she writes a check. And so do all her geriatric friends you talked into joining the board. So don't flatter yourself by confusing talent with stacking the deck. Associate Artistic Director, my ass. Gee, she bought you your title, did she have to buy you friends in school too?

ERIC. Give me back my gels. The Dolly number must be bathed in red!

JEFF. No! I've had it with you. Now listen, if your actors don't go out there happily singing and dancing their little hearts out, I'm going to happily *rip* your little heart out. Is that real enough for you?

ERIC. I am persona non grata!

*(**ERIC** exits, storming into the theatre.)*

JEFF. *(to **SCOTT**)* Now, as far as you're concerned...

SCOTT. Jeff, I had those girls bustled down to their high button shoes. The corsets and garter belts, I swear, that wasn't me. I don't know where they got them.

JEFF. Did you give my keys to "the freak?"

SCOTT. *(wincing)* Yeah.

JEFF. RULE NUMBER ONE – never give my keys to "the freak!" My keys control this theatre. The keeper of the keys is king. Never make "the freak" king. Got that?

SCOTT. But he said the Associate Artistic Director gets to use the keys.

JEFF. WELL HE'S WRONG! That title means *nothing!* Look, I know this is your first show with us, but learn from this, okay? Now do me a favor, double check so there's no more surprises. I don't know, before they go on stick your head up their skirts or something.

SCOTT. Okay.

JEFF. Okay. *(looks at **SCOTT** a second)* I'm done with you. Stand over there.

*(**SCOTT** stands where **JEFF** has pointed.)*

*(to **MIKE**)* Please, tell me you're gonna direct *Glass Menagerie* without any, ya know, mondo-bizzaro social sermon.

MIKE. Don't worry. I'll keep it simple.

JEFF. *(smiles)* Simple. I like simple. Simple is good. Simple makes me happy.

MIKE. You gotta stop letting him get to you like this. I know you think that's a bogus title you gave him, but let me tell you, if you get sick – this place is his.

JEFF. Don't worry. Everything's fine. *(gives a pep talk he's given a thousand times before)* Oh yeah, by the way, you're all doing great. I'm real proud of you. Teamwork. That's our motto. Now, let's put on a show.

(VONDO give him a "thumbs-up." JEFF exits.)

SCOTT. He's gonna have a stroke.

MIKE. No actually, it's ulcers. His doctor didn't even want him to finish the season. Doing this full time really did him in.

SCOTT. You guys full timers too?

JEANNIE. Oh God, no.

MIKE. Jeannie, Vondo and I work together at Middletown High. Jeff saw one of the shows I directed and got me over here. Then I lured them into this purgatory – and that's how we've been spending our summers for the past eight years.

SCOTT. What do you do?

MIKE. I teach English Lit. and Drama, Jeannie works in the principal's office and Vondo's the janitor.

VONDO. Also known as "The Crud Buster".

SCOTT. Hey, ah, Vondo…what time did you say the party's gonna to start tonight?

VONDO. Right after the show. You coming?

SCOTT. Yeah, I'll be there. Uh… *(looks at everyone and says very deliberately)* I'm, bringing…Ed.

MIKE. *(beat)* Okay, who's Ed?

SCOTT. Who's Ed? You mean, who is Ed? Well, Ed's…a man. Ya know, he's this guy. A *male* guy. Ya know? I'm not doing this very well, am I? Who am I kidding, your probably know already.

JEANNIE. Ya think? You're an unmarried man working in the theatre as a costume designer, who listens to non-stop Bette Midler and knows the difference between purple and aubergine. I don't know, that's some smoke screen ya got there, pal.

VONDO. *(menacing)* We got a gay costume designer?

SCOTT. *(wary)* Yeah.

VONDO. Huh. All we need now is a vending machine by the bathroom and we have arrived.

(Puts his arm around **SCOTT***, smiles and gives him a thumbs up.)*

SCOTT. *(to* **JEANNIE***)* Okay, not sure what that meant, but he's smiling, so I'll take it. God, you'd think by now at my age I'd be more comfortable...ya know...coming out, but, ...I'm from Iowa.

(JEANNIE, MIKE *and* **VONDO** *give a quiet* "Oh." *of recognition.)*

Well, I better get back in...the theatre. *(points to theatre)* I'm going back in the theatre. I didn't mean I was going back in the... *(getting slightly frustrated)* I just came out, why would I go back in?

(NOTE: To explain no live cell phone ring, since all the scenes of this play take place during a show, **VONDO***'s phone would be set to vibrate. The "buzzin'" refers the phone's vibration.)*

VONDO. OH!

(Referring to his vibrating cell phone, he hits all of his pockets to locate which pocket has the cell phone. As he's checking his pockets...)

I'm buzzin' I'm buzzin'.

(Takes out cell phone for pocket.)

(to **SCOTT***)* Wait – you gotta meet Reba. *(answers)* Hey baby! Ya called at a good time. Guess what? Ya know the new guy, Scott? Yeah, well, he just came out of the theatre from Iowa with Ed, who's this guy who's a mailman. So how'd the move go? Great. Did you get your new number? Yeah. *(points to* **SCOTT***'s clipboard)* Can you take this down? *(to* **REBA***)* Shoot. **(SCOTT** *writes)* 977-316-4149... **(SCOTT** *stops writing,* **VONDO** *looks at* **SCOTT***)* 1, 3... **(SCOTT** *quickly starts writing again.)* ... dash 1, 9. *(beat)* Cell Block C. Got it, Darlin'. Huh? No kidding! *(very proud to* **MIKE** *and* **JEANNIE***)* She's got

a window – she can see the fence. I'm real proud of ya, babe. See what good behavior'll get ya? Oh okay, I won't keep ya then. *(holds phone out)* Say bye to Reba.

MIKE & JEANNIE. Bye Reba.

*(**VONDO** stunned that **SCOTT** didn't join in, deliberately holds the phone out to him.)*

SCOTT. *(speaks into phone)* Bye Reba.

VONDO. *(to **REBA**)* Okay, baby, love ya too. A-*reba*-derci.

(Turns off phone, puts it in his pocket.)

*(to **SCOTT**)* God bless her. That woman puts the "cell" in cell phone.

SCOTT. *(tears paper off clipboard and hands it to **VONDO**)* How long has she been away?

VONDO. Sixteen years this November.

SCOTT. Wow. You've been together a long time, huh?

VONDO. *(nods)* Yeah, almost four years.

SCOTT. *(confused; offside to **MIKE**)* They met in prison?

MIKE. Oh no, she's in Montana. She was making her weekly phone call, dialed the wrong number, got Vondo and they've been together ever since.

SCOTT. *(to **VONDO**)* You've never met her?

VONDO. *(looks at him like he's crazy)* No. Why ruin a good thing?

SCOTT. *(confused)* Okay. I'm sure I'll get up to speed on this stuff. Here you go.

*(Hands paper to **VONDO** then crosses to **JEANNIE**.)*

Can you do me a favor and give these to Meredith?

JEANNIE. Sure.

*(**SCOTT** hands gloves to **JEANNIE**.)*

SCOTT. Thanks.

*(**SCOTT** exits passing **DANIEL** and **HARRIET**.)*

HARRIET. Daniel, I don't think you should be changing the choreography. Eric said to leave it be.

DANIEL. Ya know, the only reason I'm in chorus is because they need a strong dancer for the kick line. And I do strength moves no dancers would ever to do.

JEANNIE. You do lots of moves no dancers would ever do.

DANIEL. Hey, thanks. *(begins his next stupid dance move)* Five, six, seven, eight… *(practices a strength move)*

MEREDITH. *(Enters, muttering.)* I'm a pimp, I'm a pimp, was Scott just here? I'm a pimp, I'm a pimp.

(DANIEL dances by VONDO and MEREDITH and continues to dance around the stage)

I need my gloves! I'm a pimp. I'm a pimp. I'm a pimp.

(DANIEL dances by her.)

No! Don't make me look at you. I'll fall out of character! I'm a pimp. I'm a pimp. Go away!

(DANIEL dances behind the van.)

Where are my gloves?!

JEANNIE. Here! *(holds up her gloves)*

MEREDITH. *(to JEANNIE)* If I don't have my gloves, I'm not fully in character.

HARRIET. Dear, you really shouldn't cause yourself such angst. You're getting very stressed out.

MEREDITH. That's because my character is very stressed out, Harriet.

HARRIET. You know there's nothing wrong with trying to have a little fun with the role.

MEREDITH. No offense, Harriet, but I'm showing my audience an intricate person, not just some smiling cartoon. Anyone can look bouncy and happy, singing and dancing. But my Dolly is a complex human being. She's a woman who's cramped. She feels constrained, blocked. I want the audience to think she's…oh what's the word I'm looking for?

HARRIET. Constipated?

VONDO. Hey, if that's the case I can play her too.

MEREDITH. Forget it. I don't expect you to understand. *(as she puts on the gloves)* I'm a pimp, I'm a pimp...

(looks at **MIKE** *and smiles)*

(nicely) Mike, are we going to stay at the party long? I should only make an appearance. Doing this role every night takes so much out of me. I really have to come down after the show.

MIKE. That's fine with me.

MEREDITH. *(coyly)* Thanks. *(walks behind the van)* I'm a pimp, I'm a pimp, I'm a pimp...DANCE OVER THERE!

*(***DANIEL*** *does a grand jeté from behind the van.)*

JEANNIE. *(to* **MIKE***)* You're taking She-Who-Causes-Pain to the party?

VONDO. Oh! I'd rather take Ed.

MIKE. Don't start.

JEANNIE. You've watched her in action for five years and now, at the height of her tirades, you think dating her is a good idea? You're scaring me, Mike.

MIKE. Ya know, Meredith is a pretty nice person when she's not here.

JEANNIE. Ha. What brought you to that conclusion?

MIKE. Last week I went out for Chinese. I saw her there, we ate together and ended up talking for about, God, four hours. Believe it or not, there's a whole other side to her. She can be... *(a little smile)* a really sweet person.

*(***JEANNIE, VONDO*** *and* **HARRIET** *look at* **MIKE.***)*

MIKE. I've seen it.

VONDO. Mike, I've seen my foot melt away and swirl down the drain of my shower when I was dropping acid, it was fun to watch, but it wasn't real.

MIKE. We're just going to the party, that's all. I don't know what the next step will be after that.

HARRIET. Therapy, no doubt. Oh, did I say that? I'm sorry. But you know us cartoon-like little old ladies. We get ourselves all bouncy and happy singing and dancing and then senility takes over. But please dear, don't take me seriously.

(exits)

DANIEL. Ya know, I think Meredith's problem is that she feels threatened by all the competition. She can act and sing okay, but she's not a commodity. I'm a commodity. That's what my voice teacher says. He says that I should be on Broadway, but not in the chorus cuz I'm no chorus boy. I should only have leads. And that's all I've ever had. Except for now. But now doesn't count because they need my strength moves in the kick line.

*(***VONDO*** plays Smoke on the Water* quietly)*

Here, look. This is a step I made up called "soaring eagle toes".

(Starts doing the step. The step should look kinda dopey but not too ridiculous.)

See, it's a strength move. Once when I was auditioning, I was doing this step and everyone just stared at me!

*(He repeats the step over and over. ***JEANNIE*** slowly turns up the volume on ***VONDO****'s amp. ***DANIEL*** yells over the music.)*

I mean, they just sat there with their mouths open. Then they said, *(louder)* "What are you doing?" *(louder)* And I said, it's "soaring eagle toes!" It's a strength move! Only I can do it. THEY COULDN'T BELIEVE WHAT THEY WERE SEEING! I COULD TELL! AND THEN I SAID…

MEREDITH. STOP!

*(Comes out form behind the van. ***VONDO*** stops playing. Neurotic, her voice quivers.)*

I am preparing for a performance here! Can't you understand that! I can't act with this.

. (*looks at* **MEREDITH**, *then to everyone as if she wasn't*
.here) Did I mention I'm writing a new musical?

(**MEREDITH**, *exasperated, turns away.*)

I told Eric about it and he loves it! We're gonna
collaborate. He wants to produce it next season, cause
there's never been anything like it! It's about three…

ERIC. (*enters snapping his fingers*) Places, places! The
entr'acte is about to start.

(**DANIEL** *exits. As* **MEREDITH** *walks by,* **ERIC** *grabs her*
by the shoulders.)

ERIC. (*cont.*) (*points to* **MEREDITH**) You! Here. Now listen,
you can go out there an actor, or you can go out there
a singing ape. See beyond the words! (*points in her face*)
Who are you?

MEREDITH. (*on the verge of tears*) I'm Dolly Levy!

ERIC. What are you?

MEREDITH. I am a survivor!

ERIC. And what is your profession?

MEREDITH. (*grabs him by the shirt, totally in his face, and from*
the bowels of hell…) I'M A PIMP!

(*exits*)

ERIC. (*follows, calling after her in doorway.*) That's it! Now
control them! Hate them! Make them pay! (*to those left*
on stage) Hey, come on guys, it's magic time.

(**ERIC** *exits,* **JEANNIE**, **VONDO** *and* **MIKE** *follow. Lights*
dim.)

Scene II

(Music to Hello Dolly *fades. The marquiee reads: The Sound of Music plus an addition that reads: "COMING SOON, CHILDREN'S THEATRE". A poster taped onto the wall by the entrance that reads, "Auditions for* Glass Menagerie *July 10 at 7:30".* VONDO *is talking to* REBA.*)*

VONDO. Yeah, it's goin' okay. People just have opening night jitters, that's all. *(beat)* Oh, that's cause I was outta the house early this morning. Yeah. We had our first rehearsal for – *Medea. (big eyes) WHOA! (laughs, beat)* No, no, they didn't spell it wrong – it *is Medea.* Who knew?

*(*ERIC *and* JEANNIE *enter.* ERIC *holds a box marked "MEDEA" in one arm and with his other hand holds up a stocking leg that is stuffed and twisted to resemble a large intestine.)*

ERIC. Well, it's not bad. I guess when it's dipped in blood it'll look like an intestine. *(puts intestine in box)*

JEANNIE. *(reading a list)* I gotta make all of these?

ERIC. Yes! The disembowelment scene is *very* specific. Please be the same. *(puts box down)* Thank you.

VONDO. *(to* JEANNIE*)* Wanna say "hi" to Reba?

JEANNIE. *(takes phone)* Hi Reba. *(looks at list)* Do you know how to make a spleen?

*(*JEFF *enters with* MIKE *who is wearing a Nazi youth outfit and is blatantly not happy. He wears a khaki cap, shirt, tie, shorts, knees socks and a military shoe or work boots.* JEANNIE *and* VONDO *break out laughing. NOTE: the outfit does not have a swastika. This is act one of* The Sound of Music *and Rolf would not be dressed in full Nazi garb until act two.)*

VONDO. *(to* MIKE*)* What the hell are you wearing?

MIKE. I'm going on as Rolf.

VONDO. *(takes phone, to* **REBA***)* Crisis baby, gotta run. *(hangs up)* What happened?

JEFF. Billy Thurman came down with mono.

ERIC. A thirty-something year old delivery boy? I see in this production Rolf will be portrayed as an underachiever.

MIKE. Bite me.

ERIC. Don't be rude, I'm Associate Artistic Director. I outrank you.

MIKE. You sure do love that title, don't you?

ERIC. Be nice or I won't audition for *Glass Menagerie*. You need me to play Tom – you know you do.

JEFF. Knock it off, will ya? I've eaten a case of Tums today already. *(to* **MIKE***)* Look, I swear, I'll find someone to take the role tomorrow. You and Robin will be fine.

VONDO. You mean Tapestry.

JEANNIE. *(sits up)* No, not this show.

MIKE. Oh God, who is she this time? (**JEANNIE** *hands* **MIKE** *the program. Beat.)* Cheryl Streep.

(**JEANNIE** *laughs,* **MIKE** *shakes his head.)*

(to **ERIC***)* Hey Kubrick, I've got something for you. *(pulls out a CD)*

ERIC. Oh my God, is this my music?

MIKE. See if you like it. *(tosses* **ERIC** *the CD)*

ERIC. *(hands cd to* **VONDO***)* Mr. Von der Leith, I implore you, may I hear it?

(**VONDO** *takes the CD, goes to his van to play it. During the rest of the scene,* **JEANNIE** *sits on the ground and attempts to create various body organs with clay. NOTE: at no time do the organs become obscene.)*

ERIC. What is it?

MIKE. It's classical. It might be right for what you're doing. It's called, *Night On Bald Mountain*.

ERIC. *(repeats the title in a dramatic voice) Night On Bald Mountain*...I like it.

MIKE. It's by Mussorgsky.

ERIC. *(repeats the name in the same dramatic voice)* Mussorgsky…I like it.

(Music plays. ERIC's eyes light up.)

Oh my God! How wonderful! *(He enacts stabbing to the music.)* Just imagine Medea mutilating her children as blood gushes from every orifice of their bodies! This music realizes my vision! This is it!

MIKE. *(to* **VONDO***)* That's good Vondo. *(music stops)*

ERIC. Mike, I thank you. Truly I do. You have just made an important contribution to my play.

MIKE. Oh no, that's okay…keep all of the credit for yourself.

VONDO. *(comes out of the van; gives* **ERIC** *the CD)* I give it an eight. It's got a good beat and you can murder to it.

JEFF. I think it sucks.

ERIC. You'll take any chance you can to deprecate a fellow artist, won't you?

JEFF. No, just you.

ERIC. Jeffrey, we must learn to work together. You have talent! Use it! Why depict Maria as candy-coated bride of Christ, when you could portray her as a theologian anti-fascist? You wait. Between *Medea* and my collaboration with Daniel, you will see genius. I will set the stage on fire!

JEFF. Hopefully with you on it.

ERIC. I am *persona non grata*!

VONDO. What does that mean?

ERIC. It means, I am a person not wanted. *(to* **JEFF***)* See beyond the words, Mr. Director. Sing and dance no more, sing and dance no more.

*(***ERIC*** exits as* **MEREDITH** *enters. She is wearing a nun's novice habit.)*

MEREDITH. *(Shoots* **MIKE** *a nasty look. To* **JEFF**.*)* Jeff, you've got to do something. I know you told Harriet that Mother Abbess should have a Austrian accent, but every night, at the pinnacle of our scene, she looks me straight in the eye and says, *(imitates* **HARRIET**'s *accent)* "Mareea, tell mey, vaht is it you cunt face?"

JEFF. For God's sake, Meredith, I can't explain that to her!

MEREDITH. This is serious! I can't act with this.

JEFF. Okay, I'll talk to her.

   *(***MEREDITH*** sits next to* **VONDO**.*)*

JEANNIE. *(Holds up a wad of clay with a short hose sticking out of it. To* **MEREDITH**.*)* Does this look like a spleen?

   *(***ROBIN*** and* **SCOTT** *enter from the theatre.* **ROBIN**'s *playing Liesel but is not in costume yet. She wears an over-sized button down shirt.)*

SCOTT. No, I'm sorry, honey, it's not going to happen. *(goes to rack, gets sailor suit)*

ROBIN. But it's not fair. Eric said this will develop my character. It'll deepen her. It'll make her real. I'm just trying to make my character deep and real, Scott.

   (exits back into the theatre)

JEFF. What's wrong?

SCOTT. *(in a rush)* Eric got a hold of her and said since her character is sixteen going on seventeen, she's reeking with newly found sexuality. Now she wants a sexier image and asked me to make her sailor suit strapless.

JEFF. I'll talk to her.

SCOTT. Thank you. *(exits back into the theatre)*

   *(***JEFF*** follows* **SCOTT** *as* **DANIEL** *enters. He's dressed as Captain Von Trapp.* **JEFF** *turns quickly, walks the other way trying to avoid him.)*

DANIEL. Jeff! Jeff! Jeff! Jeff! *(***DANIEL*** continues barking his name until* **JEFF** *cuts him off.)*

JEFF. NO, DANIEL! No! Do you see my mouth moving? That means I'm saying something. This time try to hear it – CAPTAIN-VON-TRAPP-DOES-*NOT*-TAP-DANCE!

DANIEL. Aw, come on! The audience would really like it.

JEFF. No!

DANIEL. Then can we talk about my play?

JEFF. No.

DANIEL. Then watch this step.

JEFF. NO!

DANIEL. I can do it in "Edelweiss."

JEFF. *(as he bolts for the door)* "Edelweiss" is not a tap number!

DANIEL. *(runs after* **JEFF** *dancing all the way)* Then how about a kick line?

*(**JEFF** exits into the theatre slamming the door in* **DANIEL**'s *face.)*

VONDO. Hey Mike, did you hear that? Robin's discovering her sexuality. Know what that means? That kiss after the song? She's gonna tongue ya.

MEREDITH. Oh! You insensitive cretin. *(looks at* **DANIEL** *with contempt)* Makes me wonder if you've been taking lessons from Daniel.

DANIEL. Oh stop making such a big stink over nothing.

MEREDITH. Go to hell! It's opening night and you have the gall to give me…*your leading lady,* flowers you bought at Seven-Eleven. Jesus, why didn't you just pick me up a bouquet of Slim Jims?

JEANNIE. *(puts down whatever organ she's making)* You went to Seven-Eleven and didn't get me coffee?

MEREDITH. I'm Maria Von Trapp.

JEANNIE. You're supposed to get me coffee.

DANIEL. *(to* **JEANNIE***)* I was only there two minutes.

MEREDITH. The essence of piety and passion.

JEANNIE. You broke my coffee maker, you buy me coffee.

MEREDITH. Not to mention I'm at war with the Nazis!

JEFF. *(enters)* Has anyone seen Robin?

JEANNIE. *(points to* **DANIEL***)* He went to Seven-Eleven and didn't get me coffee.

MEREDITH. *(quickly takes off her wimple and holds it up)* I am Churchill in a habit!

JEFF. *(to* **DANIEL***)* Hey pal, you know the deal.

DANIEL. I was only there two minutes!

MEREDITH. I make myself raw for you and all you give me is convenience store carnations!

JEANNIE. I bet you reached over the coffee to get those cruddy carnations too. Didn't ya?

DANIEL. Nuh-uh. They were nowhere near the coffee.

MEREDITH . Forget about the coffee! I am trying to make a point. And my point is…

(they look at her as she tries to remember)

Roses! I'm your leading lady, I should have roses. But I guess I'm not important enough to receive roses. I mean, *(beat)* it's not as though you and I have slept together or anything. Oh, that's right, that wouldn't qualify me to be important enough to receive roses either, would it…*Mike.*

(JEFF, JEANNIE, DANIEL *and* **VONDO** *look and turn to* **MIKE.***)*

What I'm saying Daniel – is you are walking, talking proof that man evolved from swine.

(Points to **JEANNIE** *and* **VONDO***.* **VONDO** *begins to play* Smoke on the Water*.)*

These are the pig people *(points to* **DANIEL***)* and *you* are their king! *(puts her hand over the strings of* **VONDO***'s guitar stopping the sound)* Will you please stop playing that song!

VONDO. It's the only one I know.

MEREDITH . Then, do yourself a favor – expand your horizons. Learn a goddamn D chord.

---

*See Music Use Note on pg. 3.

VONDO. Hey Jeff, *(takes the wimple from* **MEREDITH** *and taps it with his foot)* ask me what I'm doing.

JEFF. What are you doing?

VONDO. I'm kicking the habit.

*(**MEREDITH** grabs her wimple from **VONDO** and smacks him with it. **JEFF** still laughing, opens the door for **MEREDITH**, she and **JEFF** exit into the theatre.)*

DANIEL. She's just mad cause I upstage her with my strength moves in the folk-dance. *(exits into the theatre)*

VONDO. *(Big smile. To* **MIKE**.*)* My, oh my. Looks like someone's been delivering more than telegrams lately.

MIKE. Don't.

VONDO. I wanna thank you, Mike. You've just opened a whole world of delivery jokes for us.

JEANNIE. Yeah, I just thought of three new words U.P.S. can stand for.

MIKE. Will you stop! And for the record, I'm not the prick she's making me out to be. I didn't have time to get her roses because I got stuck playing Knee-Sock-Boy.

VONDO. No roses. That means one thing for my poor man Mike – no overnight delivery!

*(He and **JEANNIE** laugh.)*

Ya know, I'm surprised how good this show is ending up. Katie's even coming.

MIKE. Wait, I know this – Katie's wife two.

VONDO. Katie's wife three. Carol's wife two. Debbie, or as she's known now, Sequoia Little Rain, is Frau Vondo numero uno. But Katie, yeah she was fun. I had two five or seven good years with her depending who you talk to. It started when I was at a jellyroll joint party. A jellyroll is when you take a rolling paper, sprinkle a little opiated hash over some Maui-Wowie and then, you dip it in some hash oil. Then you dip it, sprinkle it, roll it, Then you dip it, sprinkle it, roll it. Well, I lit that sucker up and BOOM! There was Katie. She walks over to me, says "hi ya, handsome" and hands me a triple shot of Quervo and a disco biscuit – for you novices, that's a Quaalude. I took one look at her in her tube top and her cut-offs, popped the lude, chased it with the Quervo and BOOM! We got married that night at The Rocky Horror Picture Show. Man, were her parents pissed. And let me tell ya, that's the only wedding I've ever been to you got to smoke the bride's bouquet. Problem was, Katie kept getting mad at me cause I couldn't remember if I divorced Debbie. Come to think of it, I'm not really sure if I divorced Katie. *(Smile fades. To* **MIKE.**) You know…I should find those papers.

MIKE. I'm telling ya, Jeannie, this guy's amazing. Show him a pot seed, he'll tell you what kind of pot it is, the part of the country it's grown in, the alkaline level of the soil, and the name of the farmer who grew it.

VONDO. Well, we're all good at something.

JEANNIE. So what made you give it up?

VONDO. One morning I woke up naked in the sink *(beat)* and my cat was shaved. But hell, I got it right now. Six times in rehab will really straighten your ass out. Nope. No more problems – except for, ever since I quit drinkin', smokin' and dopin', Yoo-hoo is my crack. *(pats his cooler)* Love it, need it, gots to have it. Steal my van, kick my cat, burn down my house, but do *not* deny me my Yoo-hoo. *(getting angst)* You think you know me? Think again. If I don't get it when I need it, I get ugly. We're talkin' pitbull with rabies ugly. *(angst)* I can handle anything you throw at me – *(deep breath)* just don't screw with my Yoo-hoo. *(Smiles. Sits on the back of the van.)*

*(***JEFF** *and* **ROBIN** *enter.* **ROBIN** *wears a white sailor suit with navy blue trim [see the movie] and has a BIG bow in her hair. Her skirt is pleated and falls at her knee. Important note:* **ROBIN** *must be wearing ankle socks and* not *tights or stockings. There is an upcoming joke and if she wears tights the joke will not go over.)*

JEFF. *(holding the script)* Vondo, will you stay on book during all of Mike's scenes, just in case.

VONDO. Sure.

JEFF. I want you two to run your lines one more time.

ROBIN. This is gonna be fun. *(sits next to **MIKE** on the bench)* My whole family will be here tonight. And know what? My temple has 112 people coming.

JEFF. Group sales. Good girl.

MIKE. Well, I hope I don't blow a line. I don't want to throw off your performance.

*(Playwright's note: At no time should the actor playing **ROBIN** act sexy during this next exchange. She does not realize the impact of what she's saying. What makes it funny is that she is the only one oblivious to what it sounds like, when everyone else is stunned. If you play it differently, it makes **ROBIN** look a little slutty, it will shift the perception of her character in the wrong way for the rest of the show, and you will totally "kill the funny" of this moment.)*

ROBIN. Oh, I'm not worried. *(very matter of fact)* I know your Rolf will be more sensual than Billy Thurman's.

*(**MIKE** and **JEFF** look at **ROBIN**.)*

(innocently) Eric says, Liesel is a sixteen year old coquette. And although she's singing that she's timid and shy, what she's really saying is, she wants be seduced.

JEFF. Ah, honey, how did Eric suggest you prepare for this role?

ROBIN. He gave me Cliff Notes to *Lolita*. *(innocently)* Eric says, I must see beyond the words. That Liesel's a survivor of puberty. She's an unbridled filly galloping through her first pasture of stallions. *(big smile to **MIKE**)* I love horses. *(to **EVERYONE**)* Eric says, Liesel is a woman-child awakening her body to...

MIKE. *(Starting to panic. Looks to **JEFF** for help.)* JEFF!

JEFF. Robin, honey, I, I think you're going a little off the deep end.

ROBIN. But, why? I've worked so hard to bring my character this far. I've deepened her.

JEFF. Yeah, I know you have, honey. And that's really quite commendable.

ROBIN. Thanks. *(Innocently smiles to* **MIKE**. *Beat.)* I'm not wearing underwear.*

MIKE. *(horrified, jumps up from bench and away from* **ROBIN***)* JESUS CHRIST!

JEFF. Ah, Robin…

MIKE. *(staring at* **ROBIN** *in horror)* SHE'S FIFTEEN!

JEFF. I know.

MIKE. I'M A TEACHER!!!!

JEFF. Calm down.

MIKE. THAT'S ILLEGAL!

VONDO. Only if you get caught.

MIKE. JESUS CHRIST!

JEFF. Now take it easy.

MIKE. TAKE IT EASY?! ARE YOU NUTS? Her father is the top criminal attorney in the state! I'm gonna be onstage while Stanley Rosenblatt, his family and the entire congregation of Temple Beth Shalom, watches his fifteen year old bare ass baby girl, thrust her newfound sexuality at me, a man twice her age, WHO'S DRESSED AS A NAZI!

JEFF. Robin…honey, I really wish you would check with me before you let someone else guide your character to such an extreme. Now, let's go back to making Liesel a sweet, innocent, young lady, okay?

ROBIN. Okay.

JEFF . Good girl. Now…go put on your panties.

ROBIN. Thanks, Jeff.

---

*Playwright's note: Say this line exactly as written. Do not add the word "any" and make it "I'm not wearing any underwear". This has been a common mistake and it trips up the laugh line.

*(***ROBIN*** *hugs* ***JEFF*** *who is uncomfortable to hug her back in her "undressed" condition raises both arms over his head.* ***ROBIN*** *exits as* ***DANIEL*** *enters.)*

MIKE. I am not doing this!

JEFF. *(with a smile and a little chuckle)* Don't worry, you'll be fine. You'll be fine and she'll be fine and I'll be fine. The only one who won't be fine – is Eric. And ya know why Eric won't be fine, Mike? Cause after the show, you and I are going to take him in the woods – AND BEAT HIM WITH A STICK! Then after that, everything will be fine. Oh yeah, by the way, you're all doing great. I'm real proud of you. Teamwork. That's our motto. Now, let's put on a show.

*(***VONDO*** *gives him a "thumbs-up".* ***JEFF*** *exits.)*

JEANNIE. *(to* ***MIKE****)* It's for one night. Don't sweat it.

MIKE. "Nazi Pervert Teacher Gropes Panty-less Von Trapp Child" – film at eleven. *(puts head in his hands)*

DANIEL. *(big smile)* Guess what? I talked to Jeff and he said I can give you my musical for you to look at for next season. Isn't that great? Eric and I already talked to the board about it and they're really interested. Finally, now people are starting to take me seriously as a playwright too. I mean, I've so many great ideas for plays and stuff. But this one's a real winner. It's called, Mime – the Musical. It's about a troupe of mimes trying to make it to the big time. Ya know, just like the movie *Fame*, except without words. And the really unique thing is, it's a musical, but nobody sings. Nobody sings with their voices, that is. They sing with their bodies. But it's not dance, it's mime. *(mimes "I'm in a box")* Ya know, I'm gonna study mime this fall. You need a lot of strength to perform mime. I'm so excited, I've even started doing the make-up palettes for the show.

JEANNIE. Why don't you just paint your face white and write "dork" on your forehead?

DANIEL. Oh, please! This is gonna be big! Everyone will know about this show cause Eric and I are gonna market it like crazy. We're gonna send flyers to clubs, schools, oh, and we're even going to have a special performance for the deaf. We're gonna have a sign interpreter sign the whole show for them.

MIKE. Daniel, why would you use an interpreter?

DANIEL. Duh. Because they're deaf.

MIKE. Yeah, I know. But you're performing the show in mime.

DANIEL. So?

MIKE. So, you don't need someone to sign it.

DANIEL. Yes I do. They can't hear.

MIKE. But no one speaks in mime.

DANIEL. I know that.

MIKE. They'll see the actors performing.

DANIEL. Well of course they will, stupid. They're not blind, they're deaf.

MIKE. My point exactly. So you don't need an interpreter.

DANIEL. Yeah, but mime is not sign language.

MIKE. I know.

DANIEL. It's mime.

MIKE. Right.

DANIEL. So they won't understand.

MIKE. They'll understand through the mime.

DANIEL. But they can't hear mime.

MIKE. No one can hear mime!

DANIEL. So they'll need an interpreter!

MIKE. NO, THEY'LL SEE IT!

DANIEL. BUT THEY WON'T *HEAR IT*, CAUSE THEY'RE *DEAF! (beat, looks at* **MIKE** *in amazement)* Boy, ya just don't get it, do ya, Mike? What's up with you? You got something against the deaf?

MIKE. NO!

DANIEL. Then why don't you want them to enjoy the theatre?

MIKE. No, I was just saying…

DANIEL. Yeah, we *know* what you were saying. Bigotry is ugly, Mike. The theatre has places for all kinds of people, but there's no room for people who hate the deaf! *(exits in a snit)*

MIKE. *(yells after him)* I DON'T HATE THE DEAF! *(desperate to* **JEANNIE***)* Please tell me you knew what I was saying.

JEANNIE. Yeah, you hate the deaf.

MIKE. I DON'T HATE THE DEAF!

JEFF. *(Enters. Confused from the theatre. To* **MIKE***.)* You hate the deaf?

MIKE. NO! Forget it!

JEFF. Okay, people, let's go.

> *(***VONDO*** enters into the theatre.)*

> *(to* **MIKE***)* Now relax, you and Robin will be fine. But just to be on the safe side, don't spin her around during the dance number.

MIKE. *(walks away from the stage door)* That's it! I am not doing this!

JEFF. Jeannie, do me a favor – go find Robin and make sure she's…ya know, fully dressed. Okay?

JEANNIE. Yeah. *(exits)*

MIKE. I mean it. I'm not going on that stage until I know she's legal.

JEFF. We'll make her legal, don't worry.

MIKE. And what the hell are you thinking? You told Daniel we might do his musical?

JEFF. Well, I had to do something. He cornered me in my office doing that *(imitates* **DANIEL***'s gestures)* "I'm in a box, I'm in a box," shit. I swear, I'm gonna kill that kid. He and Eric have been pitching the thing to the board and they're really starting to listen to them.

MIKE. So I've heard.

JEFF. Well, it won't be my problem much longer. I guess now's a good enough time as any to tell you. I'm leaving.

MIKE. What?

JEFF. I'm done, Mike. Well, I'm not done, but my wife says I'm done, my doctor says I'm done, the girl at the bagel place says I'm done. Actually, she has nothing to do with it, but she doesn't charge for cream cheese so I make her feel important. Anyway, I wanted you to be the first know. I'm outta here after this season. I called an emergency board meeting this morning and gave them my resignation.

MIKE. Oh man, that sucks. I'm sorry, Jeff.

JEFF. Yeah, well, whadda ya gonna do.

MIKE. I bet Phyllis was in her glory.

JEFF. She wasn't there. She's away this weekend. Listen, I just want to let you know, you've been really great. From the day you've stepped foot into this place you've done nothing but worked like crazy to make it better. You've always supported me when I had to fight Phyllis and the maniacs and you've been the one person I know I could trust. I can't tell you how much that's meant. That's why it really kills me that the board felt the next step was to make Eric Artistic Director.

MIKE. Are you serious? They're not really thinking that, are they? (*JEFF nods*) Jesus, you can't let that happen. If they give him this theatre, he'll kill it.

JEFF. I know.

MIKE. Well you gotta do something! I mean it. Now is no time to give in. You do anything you have to, to keep this theatre out of Eric's hands. Ya hear me, Jeff? No matter how drastic or desperate the action is, I want you to do whatever it takes and I'll stand and fight with you all the way.

JEFF. I knew I could count on you. Okay, this is where we stand. I knew I only had this once chance to strike. So I told the board I was putting my foot·down. Contrary to what they think, Phyllis doesn't run this place, I do.

(**MIKE** *gives* **JEFF** *a supportive slap on the arm.*)

And I didn't give a damn if she wasn't there, we were voting on it now.

MIKE. Good.

JEFF. So I nominated you, we voted you in and you're the new Artistic Director.

MIKE. *(front, enthusiastically)* Yes. *(quick turn to* **JEFF***)* What?

JEFF. *(shakes his hand)* You start October 16th, congratulations.

MIKE. What?

HARRIET. *(enters dressed as Mother Abbess)* Gentlemen, the temple's here and we're sold out. Mazel Tov.

JEFF. *(motions for* **MIKE** *to wait a minute)* Harriet, can I talk to you a moment?

HARRIET. What's the matter, dear?

JEFF. Well, um, I'm not exactly sure how to say this but, um, it's, your accent. You know in the scene with Meredith right before, "Climb Every Mountain?" Ahhh, how do I say this? Instead of saying, "What is it you *can't* face," it sounds more like – oh God…

HARRIET. Jeff, I think I know what you're trying to say. And let me tell you something honey, this is my fifth show with Meredith…and well…that's no accent. *(smiles, pats him on the cheek)*

(**JEFF** *looks back at* **MIKE** *and smiles.* **HARRIET** *exits into the theatre,* **JEFF** *follows her quickly to avoid* **MIKE**.)

MIKE . *(after* **JEFF***)* Whoa Jeff, wait!

ROBIN. *(Enters. With a big smile.)* Mike! Whadda ya doing out here? Come on. The overture is gonna start.

JEANNIE. *(Enters. To* ROBIN.*)* There you are. (JEANNIE *grabs* ROBIN *by the hand.)* Get in here.

(They both go into the theatre. Offstage.)

OKAY...BEND OVER. *(Sticks her head out the door. To* MIKE.*)* This is mission control, we have coverage, Houston, it's a go. *(gives a thumbs-up)*

*(*Climb Every Mountain *blares.* * *Lights fade to spot on* MIKE *bewildered. Lights fade.)*

Scene III

(Sound of Music* *fades out, the marquee now reads: Medea. An added sign reads: "Children's Theatre Presents: Cinderella". There are now two racks of costumes. One with the togas has a sign that reads: "Togas". The other reads: "Cinderella". The audition notice from the previous scene is gone. Light coming inside the theatre indicates they're in the middle of a performance.* **SCOTT** *sits in the van,* **JEANNIE** *is next to him, lying face down with her head resting on her folded arms.* **VONDO** *sits on his cooler.)*

(Playwright's note: Due to an upcoming situation, **VONDO**'s tee shirt must be white or a light color. Keep the logo small or on the back.)

SCOTT. *(laughing)* Oh my God, you're kidding!

VONDO. No, no, wait. It gets better. *(talks on phone to* **REBA***)* Ya there, babe? Okay. *(holds phone up so* **REBA** *can hear the story too)* So now we're doing, *Streetcar Named Desire.* It's dress rehearsal, at the end of some scene – Jeannie fades out the lights. Meredith goes berserk and screams, "The *only* blackout is at the end of the *rape* scene. What kind of idiot are you?"

(**MIKE** *enters during the next few lines and immediately recognizes the story.)*

SCOTT. Oh man!

VONDO. Yeah – not a good idea. Now it's opening night. We're at the end of the rape scene. Eric grabs Meredith and says the cue for the blackout, "You and I have had this date from the beginning." *(beat) Nothing.* He says it again, *(louder)* "You and I have had this date from the beginning." *Nothing.* Meredith's eyes get real big, she turns, looks up to the light booth, and there sits Jeannie – just smilin' and wavin'. *(waves)*

---

*See Music Use Note on Page 3.

JEANNIE. *(lifts head, takes* **VONDO**'s *arm that's holding the phone, and speaks into the phone)* That was the happiest day of my life. *(puts her head back down)*

SCOTT. So what happened?

MIKE. Jeff got to the light board just as Eric dropped his pants.

(**SCOTT** *and* **VONDO** *go into hysterics.*)

I'm really glad you find this funny. Are you guys gonna do this to me when I take over?

JEANNIE, VONDO & SCOTT. *(Beat. Overly sincere they nod their heads "no",* **VONDO** *hold the phone out to* **MIKE** *and shakes it back and forth as if the phone is shaking it's head "no" too.)* No! No, no, no, no, no. No.

VONDO. *(to* **REBA**) Huh? Okay babe. Catch ya later. *(holds phone up)*

JEANNIE, MIKE & SCOTT. Bye, Reba.

(**VONDO** *hangs up. Almost every time a character opens the stage door to enter or exit, we'll hear someone offstage performing* Medea. **HARRIET** *enters, we hear* **MEREDITH** *performing. She speaks all her lines with a Scottish accent.*)

MEREDITH. *(offstage)* HUSBAND! WHAT PAIN YE HAVE CAUSED ME! I SCREAM NOW, AS I DID WHILE BIRTHING YOUR UNWANTED OFFSPRING!

HARRIET. *(closes the door)* My God, this show is awful.

SCOTT. I'm confused. Isn't she supposed to have a Greek accent?

JEANNIE. She thinks she does.

HARRIET. Are you two alright? You look exhausted.

SCOTT. We've been here since seven.

HARRIET. My goodness, why so early?

SCOTT. Nobody expected *Cinderella* to go over so well.

JEANNIE. *(lifts her head, her eyes half closed)* Jeff added shows at eleven, two, and five. Then we do whatever the hell the evening show is. At least we have it easy now. Eric wants only one light cue at the death scene. So until then, we get to sit here. *(Her pathetic cheer trails off as she puts her head down.)* Yaaaaay.

HARRIET. *(to* **MIKE***)* So how are you holding up?

MIKE. Eric's going ballistic screaming to the board he wants to have a say in next season. Phyllis thinks we should be co-artistic directors. And Jeff keeps on me every second not to give them an inch. Jesus, no wonder he's got ulcers. Now I know what I'll be like in twelve years.

JEANNIE. *(lifts head)* Ha. Try August.

HARRIET. *(to* **MIKE***)* Should I ask?

MIKE. Yeah, I told him I'd do it. But now I'm directing two shows back to back.

JEANNIE. What?

MIKE. I'm gonna finish directing *Oklahoma* for Jeff. Before he jumps ship, he wants to take two weeks, rebudget, put together a proposal and see if he can get some other source of funding. That way I won't have to put up with Eric, Phyllis or things like –

(Instantaneously **ROBIN** *enters opens the theatre door and immediately we hear offstage.)*

MEREDITH. *(offstage)* SPEW YOUR VOMIT YOU WORTHLESS BAG O'PUKE!

*(***MIKE** *gestures to the door.)*

ROBIN. *(wearing a pink toga and a laurel of flowers)* Hey Scott, I'm done with my scene. Can you help me with my murder costume?

SCOTT. Sure. This is such a pain in the ass. Ya know how Eric had me line all the kid's costumes with blood packets? Now, nobody can sit down before they get killed or they'll pop. *(goes to costume rack.)*

MIKE. *(aside to* **ROBIN***)* Hey Robin, are you going out with us after the show?

ROBIN. Yeah, I was gonna.

MIKE. Can you do me a favor and not talk about *Glass Menagerie?* Only the people that got parts know who's in the cast. So, I don't want to talk about it until I've officially announced it. Okay?

ROBIN. Okay.

(as **MIKE** *turns* **ROBIN** *innocently but loudly says)*

Thanks again for letting me play Laura! I can't wait! It'll really increase my range as an actress. *(to* **EVERYONE***)* I get to limp.

*(***SCOTT** *and* **ROBIN** *exit to the trailer.)*

JEANNIE. *(sits up, to* **MIKE***)* You didn't give the part to Meredith?

MIKE. No.

JEANNIE. Does she know this?

MIKE. No.

JEANNIE. Can we watch when you tell her?

MIKE. Stop! She is gonna be crushed. You have no idea how bad she wanted this part. It's all she's talked about for weeks. And you should've seen her at auditions. She thought she nailed it. And, she wasn't bad, but, she just wasn't right for the role. No matter how I looked at it, she was just too…

HARRIET. *(with a sarcastic little smile)* Tall?

*(***MIKE** *turns to* **HARRIET.***)*

You don't think she's too tall, dear?

MIKE. No.

HARRIET. Well, if she's not too tall whatever could it be?

MIKE. You're gonna make me say it, aren't you? Fine. She's too old. Is that what you want to hear?

HARRIET. *(with a sweet smile)* Every waking moment, dear.

MIKE. I mean, Laura's in her twenties – tops. So Meredith really didn't stand much of a chance.

VONDO. Robin just got the lead in *West Side Story* too. I'm telling ya, this kid is kickin' ingénue butt.

MIKE. I know. And the funny thing is, she has no idea how talented she is.

JEANNIE. Yeah well, Meredith does. Especially since the review of *Sound Of Music* said Robin was outstanding but Meredith played Maria more like Attila the Nun.

MIKE. That review was pretty unfair.

JEANNIE. No it wasn't. She didn't listen to Jeff's direction and she got exactly what she deserved. Despite it all, I feel bad for her. This place may be the starting gate for Robin, but it's the last lap for Meredith.

(DANIEL enters. He's playing Medea's husband and wears a toga and a head laurel.)

DANIEL. Guess what? I improvised a little dance with Meredith. I spun her around and put her into a dip. Boy, did it enhance her character! You could really see the tension in her face. Ya know, before the season ends, Eric and I are gonna do a workshop production of our show, Mime. This means I'm gonna have to prepare myself mentally for the characters. So Eric suggested from now on, unless I'm onstage, I shouldn't talk. I should only communicate through mime.

JEANNIE. Oh, Daniel, that's really not a good idea.

DANIEL. Duh. Sure it is. It's a great way to…

JEANNIE. *(cuts him off quick)* Daniel! I'm gonna try to help you. I'm gonna do something I avoid doing at all costs. I'm gonna talk to you. To be blunt, I hate you. I hate you, and I hate mime. And I'm not alone. *(beat)* We have a club. We meet on Mondays. We pay dues. We have bake sales. We go on bus trips – ⟨⟩ we see *Phantom.* And guess what? We all ha⟨⟩ And we're getting bigger every str⟨⟩ me on this, take the mime idea an⟨⟩ toilet. Cause there are people ou⟨⟩ hurt you – they wanna hurt ya ba⟨⟩ now, you are looking at the Gr⟨⟩ all.

(DANIEL *looks at* JEANNIE *and mimes a single tear falling from his eye. He puts his index finger beneath his eye, makes a boo-boo face, and traces the tear rolling down his cheek.*)

JEANNIE. Stop it!

(DANIEL *repeats the action quicker this time.*)

STOP IT!

(JEANNIE *crosses as* DANIEL *follows miming "You broke my heart." He takes his two hands, cups them so they make a heart. He puts them on his chest, then separates his two hands as the broken heart.*)

GET AWAY FROM ME!

ERIC. (*enters from the theatre, holding a bloody leg*) Quiet! There is a performance going on in here!

MEREDITH. (*wailing offstage*) OOOOOOOOOOOOOOOOOO OOOOOOOOOHHHHHHH!!

ERIC. You almost made me miss my favorite line. Now shut up! (*goes back in, door closes*)

(DANIEL *puts his finger up to his mouth and mimes "SHHHHH!" then "zipper my lips" and continues various other mime actions – i.e. walking a dog, pulling a rope, going down stairs*)

JEANNIE. (*watches* DANIEL *miming*) Vondo, start your van and run him over.

VONDO. Come on, Honey. Let's go in the theatre so you can laugh at the actors. Won't that be fun?

(JEANNIE *grabs her staple gun and shoots staples at* DANIEL, *who mimes shooting in a gun duel.* VONDO *grabs* JEANNIE *and exits into the theatre as* DANIEL *follows passing* JEFF *and* ERIC *as they enter.*)

MEREDITH. (*offstage, sings in frantic operatic voice*) LA! LA, LA, LA, *LA!* LA, LA, LA, *LA!* LA, LA, LA, *LA!*

akes his head in disbelief) Wow. (*he closes the door*)

powerful, huh?

JEFF. Oh, it's making an impact, all right. *(to* **MIKE** *as he points to theatre door)* This is all because I listened to Phyllis and let Eric pick one show this season. Remember that, heed it, tattoo it on your ass.

ERIC. Laugh now but wait till tomorrow. The box office will be mobbed!

MIKE. I think the only mob you'll see is the one running you out of town.

ERIC. Don't talk down to me, peasant. You're not Artistic Director yet. Remember, Aunt Phyllis has made it quite clear that she wants her money to be used for the development of new works, especially mine.

JEFF. Yeah well, after she gets a gander of that – I won't be surprised if she turns this place into a Jiffy Lube.

MIKE. And can't you ever be accurate? Medea only has two sons. Why do you have her as the mother of six?

ERIC. Because this is *my* version! Besides, we had all those Von Trapp kids left over. Don't worry Mike, Meredith will be brilliant in the murder scene – I've instilled her with rage. I just informed her you screwed her out of her part in *Glass Menagerie*.

MIKE. You told her? You bastard.

*(**MIKE** exits into the theatre. **ROBIN** enters from the trailer. She's is wearing a white toga. This toga* must *be white. She wears a laurel of white flowers in her hair.)*

MEREDITH. *(offstage)* HERE KITTY, KITTY, KITTY, KITTY, KITTY! *(door closes)*

ERIC. Ah, here's my little sacrificial lamb. My dear, are you mentally prepared to have your insides brutally eviscerated from your body and spattered upon the stage for all the world to see?

ROBIN. *(with a smile)* Okay.

VONDO. *(goes to the van, picks up a small bag)* Hey Robin, I have a little opening night present for you.

ROBIN. *(takes bag)* This is for me? You didn't have to do that! Vondo, you're so nice! *(takes the bag and pulls out a*

small white teddy bear with a Greek laurel wreath on its head)
Oh my gosh, he's so cute! Look! *(shows it to* **HARRIET***)*

HARRIET. Oh, isn't he precious!

ROBIN. Vondo, I really, really love him! You are the sweetest person in the whole wide world!

VONDO. Well, break a leg.

ROBIN. Thanks!

(She runs, throws her arms around **VONDO** *'s neck and hugs him big. They separate and all of* **ROBIN** *'s blood packets have popped. She and* **VONDO** *are covered in blood.)*

OH MY GOD!

VONDO. *(Seeing he too is covered in blood, he just screams.)* AHHHHHHHHHHHHHHHHHH!

ERIC. OH MY GOD! *(to* **JEFF***)* GET SCOTT! HURRY, GET SCOTT!

*(***JEFF** *exits to the trailer.* **VONDO***, eyes bulging, looking at his shirt, trembling in fear.)*

ROBIN. THIS IS SO GROSS! *(She puts her bear down.)*

HARRIET. *(Sees* **VONDO** *in shock. Speaks deliberately.)* Vondo, honey, it's okay. It was her costume. It wasn't real.

*(***JEFF** *and* **SCOTT** *barrel in from the trailer)*

SCOTT. *(sees* **ROBIN***)* OH SHIT!

*(***SCOTT** *runs over to the rack of costumes and frantically searches through it.)*

ROBIN. *(crying)* I popped!

ERIC. FOR GOD'S SAKE DO SOMETHING!

JEFF. Can you put another toga on her?

SCOTT. No. She won't bleed when she gets stabbed!

ERIC. SHE HAS TO BLEED WHEN SHE GETS STABBED!

JEFF. Well, put a sheet on her or something.

SCOTT. She'll seep right through it. Then she'll be bleeding before she gets stabbed.

ERIC. SHE CAN'T BLEED BEFORE SHE GETS STABBED!

SCOTT. I KNOW THAT!

ERIC. WELL, YOU'RE THE GODDAMN COSTUME DESIGNER! DO SOMETHING!

SCOTT. NOW IS NOT THE TIME TO PISS ME OFF, ERIC!

ERIC. Take this situation and create with it! Use it! Use It!

SCOTT. SHUT UP!

*(**SCOTT** exits to the trailer, **JEANNIE** and **MIKE** enter from the theatre.)*

MIKE. *(rushing out)* Hey, keep it down. We can hear you in... *(sees **ROBIN**)* Jesus!

JEANNIE. Oh my God! What happened?

VONDO. I popped her prematurely.

*(**JEANNIE** helps clean up **ROBIN**. **MIKE** runs over to a laundry-type bag or basket by the rack and finds a towel or other things to wipe the blood off Robin. He hands them to **JEANNIE** and **HARRIET** but he does not wipe the blood off **ROBIN** as that would be inappropriate. Playwright's note: If there is blood splattered on the floor, at no time should any actor wipe the floor of the stage. Remember, they are in a parking lot and would not wipe the asphalt.)*

HARRIET. Would you believe this is the result of a harmless little thank you hug?

ROBIN. *(crying)* I didn't mean it! I really didn't mean it!

ERIC. Remain calm, little one. *(screams)* WE MUST REMAIN CALM!

EVERYONE. SHHHHHHHHHH!

HARRIET. *(wiping the blood off **ROBIN**)* It's okay honey. I'm sure Scott can fix this.

JEANNIE. *(wiping the blood off **ROBIN**)* Yeah, he'll have you looking as good as new...in about a week.

VONDO. I'm so sorry, Robin. I really am. Please don't cry. God, I feel like I just shot the Easter Bunny.

*(**SCOTT** enters running.)*

SCOTT. Okay, I need help.

(They huddle around **ROBIN** *and begin to dress her.)*

ERIC. What the hell is that?

ROBIN. Oh, Scott...please say you're kidding.

SCOTT. Let's just see how it looks.

MIKE. Are you sure about this?

SCOTT. *(frantically dresses her)* Work with me, people. I have thirty seconds to make a costume, so just work with me, goddamnit! *(beat)* Well, I'll admit, it's not the correct time period. But it'll have to do.

(They step back to reveal **ROBIN** *wearing a trash bag with some kind of Greek toga belt.)*

ERIC. She can't wear that.

ROBIN. I look stupid.

SCOTT. Well, that's all I've got!

ROBIN. *(in tears)* Oh God, I used my real name for this show.

ERIC. THIS IS ABSURD! Nobody will see her bleed when she gets stabbed!

SCOTT. Well I don't hear you coming up with a solution! *(thinks)* Look, Robin, when you get stabbed, rip the bag – like you're in pain or something. That way people will see the blood.

ERIC. Yes! That's it! But don't think of it as ripping the bag, think of it as shedding your skin. It's a re-birth! Understand?

ROBIN. *(crying)* No.

ERIC. It'll deepen her. Understand?

ROBIN. *(crying)* No.

ERIC. Good enough, get in there. *(to* **VONDO***)* You. Go with her and cue the music. *(proclaims)* We will have murder. *(to* **ROBIN** *as she walking)* Now take this and use it! See beyond the words, little one. See beyond the words.

*(***ROBIN** *nodding "yes" gives a little sniffle/sob as she exits into the theatre.* **VONDO** *and* **SCOTT** *follow her.)*

ERIC. Congratulations, all! We've taken a negative and made it a positive! That garbage bag has become a part of who she is. Now, no one will ever even notice.

(**MEREDITH** *enters holding a head. She wears a toga, her hair is done like a Greek goddess She stays in character and continues to speak with a Scottish accent.*)

MEREDITH. Why is me daughter wearing a trash bag?

JEFF. There was a little mishap.

ERIC. Don't tell her that!

JEFF. Fine! You explain it. Bye-bye.

(**JEFF** *exits into the theatre.*)

ERIC. *(to* **MEREDITH***)* There was no mishap! As she dies, your daughter will shed her skin. It's a re-birth.

MEREDITH. That's ridiculous!

ERIC. Who are you? Tell me who you are!

MEREDITH. I'm Medea, a Greek heroine with serial killer tendencies.

ERIC. Right! And this is your new motivation for murdering your children.

MEREDITH. But ye can't change me motivation right a'fore me big scene!

ERIC. Oh for God sakes, TAKE IT AND USE IT!

MEREDITH. I can't act with this. *(as she opens door to theatre and exits…)*

DANIEL. *(offstage)* CHILDREN, YOUR MOTHER ARRIVES! TIME TO SLAUGHTER THE YAK.

ERIC. *(sigh of relief)* Well, I guess every show has to have at least one little disaster to truly make it a success.

VONDO. *(enters)* Hey Eric, did you put the CD in the sound booth? It's not in the player.

ERIC. What? Oh my God, don't tell me that! Oh my God! I'm sure I put it in the booth. Oh my God!

MIKE. Okay, don't panic. Start looking for it!

ERIC. We've gotta find it or my play will be ruined!

(From this point on, the action and lines happen very fast. Everyone searches for the CD.)

VONDO. Harriet, can you hold the door? I gotta hear my cue.

HARRIET. Sure, honey. *(She opens the theatre door and will continue to hold it until the end of the scene.)*

MEREDITH. *(offstage)* COME TO ME HUSBAND. KISS ME! TELL ME YE LOVE ME!

MIKE. *(searching a prop box)* Is it in your backpack?

ERIC. I DON'T KNOW! *(gets his backpack and searches through it)* Oh my God! The entire fate of this show depends on that music!!!

VONDO. *(nervous)* Oh boy, I'll check the booth again.

(runs into the theatre as **HARRIET** *holds the door)*

MIKE. *(yells after him)* Tell Jeff to cover the lights.

MEREDITH. *(offstage)* NAY! NAY! NAY I SAY! YOUR LOVE SCORNS ME!

JEANNIE. *(to* **ERIC***)* Did you listen to it today?

ERIC. *(stops)* THE VAN!

(They bolt over to the van and start searching it frantically. **JEANNIE** *jumps into the front.)*

MEREDITH. *(offstage)* VENGEANCE BE ME LOVER, ABSOLUTION BE ME FRIEND!

JEANNIE. *(from inside the van)* It's not in the player!

VONDO. *(enters)* It's not in the booth.

ERIC. SHIT! *(things fly out of the van)*

MEREDITH. *(offstage)* SWEET REVENGE THE DAY IS YOURS! HEAR ME SING YOUR SONG!

VONDO. *(nervously as he runs to the van)* HEY GUYS, SHE'S GONNA GIVE ME THE CUE!

ROBIN. *(offstage)* MOTHER! WHY DO YE LOOK SO COLD? MOTHER! WHY DO YE LOOK SO QUEER?

ERIC. FIND IT! THERE HAS GOT TO BE MUSIC!

(VONDO *runs over to the van, grabs his guitar and amp and unnoticed by all except* **HARRIET**, *dashes back into the theatre. Things continue to fly from the van.*)

MEREDITH. *(offstage)* ME CHILDREN, THERE IS ONLY ONE WAY TO ATONE FOR YOUR SINS!

ERIC. SHIT! THE NEXT LINE'S THE CUE!!!

JEANNIE. GOT IT!

ERIC. GIMME!

(**JEANNIE** *throws* **ERIC** *the CD just as* **MEREDITH** *gives the cue.* **ERIC** *bolts to the doorway.*)

MEREDITH. *(offstage)* DAUGHTERS AND SONS, *YE MUST DIE!*

(*As* **ERIC** *hits the doorway,* **VONDO** *inside, plays* Smoke on the Water* *– only the first four measures, over and over.* **ERIC** *freezes in his tracks. We hear* **MEREDITH** *over the music.*)

MEREDITH. *(offstage)* WHO WILL DANCE WITH ME DAGGER NEXT? YOU, DAUGHTER?

ROBIN. *(offstage)* NO MOTHER! NO! AHHHHHHHH!

DANIEL. *(offstage)* YOU'RE A DEMON WOMAN! YOU'RE A DEMON WOMAN!

(**ERIC** *turns slowly, and walks out of the doorway.* **JEANNIE** *walks to the van and sits.*)

MEREDITH. *(offstage)* YES! THAT'S RIGHT! SHED YOUR SKIN! SHED YOUR SKIN AND DIE!!!!

(**MIKE** *sits next to* **JEANNIE**. **HARRIET**, *still holding the door, tries to suppress her laughter.*)

ROBIN. *(offstage, wailing.)* MAAAAA-MAAAAA!!!

(**JEFF** *enters from the theatre, kinda in a daze, not really looking at anything. He has his bottle of Tums in his right hand and as he walks, he slowly turns the bottle over so a Tum falls in his left hand. He stands next to*

---

*See Music Use Note on pg. 3.

MIKE, *who is on* **JEFF** *'s right and is also kinda in a daze, not really looking at anything.* **JEFF,** *without looking at* **MIKE** *hands him the bottle.* **MIKE,** *without looking at* **JEFF,** *takes the bottle in his left hand, he slowly turns the bottle over so a Tum falls in his right hand.* **JEANNIE** *takes a deep breath and then lies back in the van.* **ERIC,** *defeated, is sitting on the ground, looking at the CD in his hand. And just as the lights begin to fade,* **JEFF** *and* **MIKE,** *not looking at each other and still staring off in disbelief, simultaneously put their Tums in their mouths. Fade to black.)*

(END OF ACT I)

ACT II

Scene I

(Lights up. Time: right before Act II. The marquee reads: Now Playing – Oklahoma. An added sign reads: Little Red Riding Hood. There are two racks with costumes, one with a sign that reads: Oklahoma, closest to the stage door. The other sign reads: Little Red. Next to the stage door is a barrel big enough to sit on. The word "PICKLES" is stenciled in black letters. JEANNIE lies in the van, legs hanging over the edge. She's dressed in a gingham prairie-dress and her hair is in braids. She is tired, cranky and gets crankier as the scene progresses. SCOTT is sitting next to her with his eyes closed. VONDO stands by the door wearing a tee shirt and cow-pants that are held up by suspenders and some kind of footwear that represents hoofs. He is playing the back end of a cow, and is subtly practicing his "hoof moves" (i.e. like a dog does with his back legs to kick dirt.) MIKE enters but only sticks his head out from the theatre door. He has begun the take over of the theatre and we should see that it's already beginning to take its toll on him.)

MIKE. *(sticks his head out the door)* Act II, Party Scene, ten to places. Let's move it folks.

SCOTT. *(nudges JEANNIE)* Jeannie! JEANNIE!

JEANNIE. *(sits up abruptly)* What! I hate you. I hate you with the white-hot intensity of the sun.

SCOTT. Oh, I love this on the edge, country-bumpkin thing ya got going on. You're like Laura Ingalls with cramps.

(JEFF enters wearing slightly more casual clothes than in previous scenes.)

JEFF. Hey, anyone going out after the show?

SCOTT. *(deliberately to* **JEFF***)* We'd love to but we can't. We gotta be here at seven – A. M. Thank you!

JEFF. And don't be late, we've got two day care centers coming.

SCOTT. God, you're killing me with this, Jeff. I can't even think straight.

JEANNIE. *(with her eyes closed)* Of course you can't, you're gay. *(giggles, slaps* **SCOTT***'s knee)*

SCOTT. *(smiles at* **JEANNIE***)* Oh Vondo, I forgot.

*(***SCOTT** *walks over to the rack.).*

Look what I have.

(He holds up a very ornate crown.)

VONDO. Cool! It's my crown for Sleeping Beauty. *(puts crown on his head)* This has been a good summer for me acting wise. I'm in this show, I'm playing the King in *Sleeping Beauty,* and I just got cast as Glad Hand in *West Side Story.* Yeah, it's pretty cool.

*(***DANIEL** *enters. He's playing Will Parker and wears cowboy garb. He's does various cowboy choreography, stops in front of* **SCOTT** *and performs a cowboy high-kick. He "Skips to My Lou" behind the van.* **VONDO** *will observe the following exchange, occasionally practicing a subtle hoof move.)*

SCOTT. If he doesn't stop that we're gonna to have to call this show "Okla-homo."

JEFF. Actually, we don't know if he's gay or straight.

SCOTT. Oh come on!

JEFF. No, we're not sure.

(Beat. **SCOTT** *and* **JEANNIE** *simultaneously.)*

SCOTT. I hope he's not gay.   **JEANNIE.** I hope he's not straight.

(They look at each other.)

JEANNIE. Well, we don't want him.

SCOTT. Well we don't want him either.

JEANNIE. Tough. Our side has enough assholes. You want equality, pick up the slack.

SCOTT. Hey we have our share of idiots too, ya know.

JEANNIE. Okay, name one. *(snapping her fingers)* Come on, come on, come on…

SCOTT. *(getting angst)* Ahhh…stop! I can't think that fast!

JEANNIE. Too bad. Till you come up with some, he's gay by default.

SCOTT. Jeff, is Daniel straight or gay?

JEFF. Is this really that important to you?

JEANNIE. We have Eric.

JEFF. *(to SCOTT)* Hey pal, he's yours.

SCOTT. OH, OKAY! But, if I think of someone – you get him back.

JEANNIE. Fine. But here are the rules – one: he has to be a public figure who's an idiot and/or bastard and two: he has to be gay-approved by the Official Chapter of the Friends of Dorothy.

SCOTT. You keep saying "he". Why does it have to be a man?

JEANNIE. Because all lesbians are cool. Jesus dude, I know you're from Iowa but at least read your manual.

(MIKE enter but only sticks his head out from the theatre door.)

MIKE. *(annoyed)* Excuse me, I've got half a cow in here.

VONDO. Oh shoot! *(Runs to theatre door with crown still on his head.)*

SCOTT. *(running after VONDO)* Wait, wait, wait, wait ,wait!

(SCOTT grabs the crown off his head just as VONDO exits through the theatre door. He runs to the rack to put the crown back. As he does…)

JEANNIE. *(smiling to SCOTT)* You got five minutes, tick, tock, tick, tock…

SCOTT. *(as he runs into the theatre)* Oh shut up!

(SCOTT and MIKE exit in to the theatre, with MIKE closing the door. DANIEL enters from around the corner, walks over to JEANNIE and mimes, very clearly, to her that he is sewing a button on his cuff. The following should flow smoothly and quickly.)

JEANNIE. You're writing a novel…

    (DANIEL shakes his head "no", mimes quicker.)

…you're fixing a flat?

    (DANIEL mimes bigger.)

You're baking a pie…

    (DANIEL mimes frantically.)

…you're snow mobiling.

    (DANIEL, exasperated, stamps his foot and exits into the theatre.)

JEFF. *(to JEANNIE.)* He was sewing a button.

JEANNIE. I know.

    (MIKE enters.)

MIKE. Jeannie, let's go! *(sees pickle barrel)* Oh crap! What's the pickle barrel doing here?

JEANNIE. *(with her back to MIKE as she puts on her hat)* I dunno.

MIKE. Well, it's gotta be on stage for dance number. Bring it on instead of your basket.

JEANNIE. No.

MIKE. Why not?

JEANNIE. Cause, *(turns revealing that she wears a "hick" looking country straw hat)* I'll look stupid.

MIKE. Just walk on, put it down and walk off. No one will notice.

JEANNIE. It's the big party! All the girls are bringing their pretty little picnic baskets – but not me. I'm the socially challenged inbred. I trot in there with a pickle barrel. *(in a hick accent)* Hoo-wee! Now don't you fellers go payin' no mind to them purty baskets filled with them homemade pree-serves. Lookie here! I done got me a pickle barrel.

MIKE. Take it.

JEANNIE. No!

JEFF. JEANNIE! *(opens the theatre door and holds it for* **JEANNIE** *)*

JEANNIE. Goddamn it! *(picks up barrel and lugs it to the stage door)*

SCOTT. *(enters running)* Hold it! *(points at* **JEANNIE** *)* That gay guy who married Liza!

JEANNIE. Which one?

(beat)

SCOTT. Shit.

(exits back around the corner to the trailer)

*(***JEANNIE** *exits into the theatre with barrel.* **MIKE** *crosses to the van, going over the papers with* **JEFF**. **ERIC** *and* **ROBIN** *enter from the trailer.* **ROBIN** *is playing Laurey,* **ERIC** *is playing Jud, both are dressed for the party.)*

(Playwright's note: It is mandatory that the director and actors playing **ERIC** *and* **ROBIN** *read the playwright's notes in the back of the script regarding this scene. While the general note is for* **ERIC** *not to play this exchange dirty, there are specific elements both the actors and director need to know. Thank you for obliging.)*

ERIC. No, no, you're resisting! See beyond the words. You're Laurey, I'm Jud, you're the cornfield, I'm the farmer. My goal is to get you plowed. When the time is right, I'll sprinkle my seeds into your furrow. Of course, once I see you sprouting, my natural instinct is to reap you – but that won't happen till the harvest. Understand?

ROBIN. *(confused)* No. *(***ROBIN** *tries very hard to concentrate and understand* **ERIC**.*)*

ERIC. These people are products of their environment.
Take Curly. You think he's the show's cowboy hero?
Ha! He'll rope you down, tie you up, take his branding
iron and ram it in your hide. Jud is far more genteel.
As far as he's concerned, once your kernels have fully
developed, he just takes you home and shucks you.
Get it?

ROBIN. No.

ERIC. *(sighs)* Then think of our characters as farm tools.
I'm a spade and you're a hoe...

JEFF. WILL YOU LEAVE HER ALONE! You're gonna have
her on Prozac before her first prom. *(to* **ROBIN***)* You
better get inside, honey. Knock 'em dead.

ROBIN. Thanks, Jeff!

JEFF. *(as she passes him)* You're wearing underwear?

ROBIN. *(big smile)* Yeah. *(exits into the theatre)*

JEFF. *(looks at* **MIKE***)* Welcome to my world. *(exits into the
theatre)*

MIKE. *(to* **ERIC***)* Look – the last time you tried to change her
character, I almost did time. I'm the director. This is
my show. I call the shots. Leave her alone.

ERIC. You stifle me!

MIKE. I wish!

*(**ERIC** heads for the theatre as **JEANNIE** enters. The next
two lines are done in passing.)*

ERIC. *(sarcastically as he approaches* **JEANNIE***)* Nice hat.

JEANNIE. *(gives* **ERIC** *the finger and says flatly)* See beyond the
words.

*(**ERIC** exits into the theatre.)*

JEANNIE. Dumb-ass show. You better be picking decent
shows next year. Jeff said you're thinking about doing
Cats. Do that and I'll quit. Last thing I need is spending
the summer with singin' pussy-people poppin' out of
trash cans.

MIKE. Tone down the crankiness, will ya.

JEANNIE. Oh no, I think Meredith gets to wear the "cranky crown." She's making everyone miserable cause you didn't give her that goddamn part. Plus, she's pissin' up a storm cause you didn't get her roses for this show either – nice move.

MIKE. I've been here, in meetings since eight a.m.

JEANNIE. Well, maybe if you can get your head outta Phyllis' ass for five minutes you can tell Nurse Ratchet to knock it off cause she's acting like a maniac. Just dump her, will ya?

MIKE. Right, first I don't give her the part, now you want me break up with her?

JEANNIE. (big smile) Okay. God, when did you get so wimpy.

MIKE. I'll take care of it as soon as things calm down. Shouldn't you be human? I heard Daniel brought you coffee.

JEANNIE. Oh yeah. After six weeks, today he walks in and hands me a twenty-ounce cup of cinnamon banana macadamia nut – decaf. (looks at MIKE) Who the fuck drinks banana coffee?

MIKE. I don't need this.

JEANNIE. I hope Daniel gets scabies.

MIKE. Get your basket!

JEANNIE. Ya sure you don't want me pushing a wheelbarrow with a sign that says "dung for sale?"

MIKE. God almighty, take a pill! (exits into the theatre)

SCOTT. (enters running) I got it – and I know I'm right. Frank Sinatra Jr.

JEANNIE. No way.

SCOTT. (very confident) Ah, yes way. I read in his dad's biography, he had an affair with Joey Heatherton.

(SCOTT nods his head confidently. JEANNIE smirks.)

What?

JEANNIE. Joey Heatherton's a woman.

SCOTT. 'Fraid not, he's one of the "Rat Pack".

JEANNIE. That's Joey Bishop.

SCOTT. Shit.

(DANIEL *enters from the theatre as* SCOTT *exits to the trailer.*)

JEANNIE. Glenn Close is a woman.

SCOTT. Fuck you. *(exits to the trailer)*

(DANIEL *points to her; mimes sewing a button again.*)

JEANNIE. You're petting a squirrel?

(DANIEL *stamps his foot; mimes.*)

You're Betsy Ross?

(DANIEL *does "on the nosy" gestures, "come on" then mimes again.*)

You're loading a musket.

(DANIEL *shakes his head.*)

You're fighting the British.

(*mimes sewing gigantically*)

You're crossing the Delaware.

(DANIEL, *raises both fists, shakes them, mimes screaming, then sits on* VONDO's *cooler.* JEANNIE *exits skipping happily into the theatre passing* MIKE *and* JEFF *as they enter.*)

JEFF. *(annoyed)* Why does it always happen during a performance?

MIKE. I ordered six bails of hay, I don't know why there's only five.

JEFF. I told you, you have to double check everything because if there's a mistake, it's gonna fall on you.

MIKE. I know, but this is not helping me now. We need something about this high *(gestures about the height of* VONDO's *cooler)* to stick under the hay. I think you'll see it in the wagon then. (MIKE *exits around the corner to the trailer.*)

JEFF. All right. Crap!

*(**DANIEL**, holding his lasso, walks over and taps **JEFF** on the shoulder.)*

What?

(Indicates he has idea by miming a light bulb over his head. Then he mimes being cold by shivering.)

Let me make this clear – the surrey with the fringe on top can easily do a drive by. So if you want to live to doe-see-doe another day, I suggest you tell me what you want!

*(**DANIEL** stamps his foot, walks over and points to **VONDO**'s cooler and shivers.)*

The cooler?

*(**DANIEL** nods "yes.")*

Yeah, I guess we could use that. *(calls offstage to **MIKE**)* Hey Mike, this good?

MIKE. *(sees it as he enters)* Yeah, that'll do. *(takes cooler and exits into the theatre)*

*(**DANIEL** holds his free hand up to ear to mime that he wants to hear something from **JEFF**.)*

JEFF. *(reluctantly)* Okay, the idea didn't suck.

*(**DANIEL** clutches his heart.)*

Get away from me.

*(**DANIEL** crosses and sits by the van. **HARRIET**, **ROBIN** and **MEREDITH** enter from the theatre. **MEREDITH** is playing Ado Annie and **HARRIET** is playing Aunt Eller.)*

MEREDITH. You don't get it. You just don't get it. Ado Annie is a survivor.

ROBIN. Eric says to fully develop your character an actor has to use dangerous obstacles they survive in everyday life. I'm doing that and it really helps. Today I survived a manicure and tomorrow – I'm surviving brunch. *(puts her basket on the prop table, grabs a small bouquet of violets and exits into the theatre)*

HARRIET. I think actresses use the survivor term a bit too much. It's turned into quite a cliché.

MEREDITH. But Ado Annie has tons of survivor qualities. And what she doesn't have, I supplement from my own life.

JEFF. What terrible thing has ever happened to you that qualifies you to be called a survivor?

MEREDITH. Well for starters, let's try that last embarrassing production you directed. Eric was right, I should have a shirt made that says: I survived *The Sound of Music*.

JEFF. Too bad you won't be wearing one that says: "I survived *The Glass Menagerie*." Oh that's right, before you can survive the show, you have to survive the audition.

(**MEREDITH** *slams basket on the prop table exits in the theatre. As* **JEFF** *and* **HARRIET** *exit to the trailer…*)

HARRIET. Well, I hope she has to cry in her next scene.

JEFF. Was I too tough on her?

HARRIET. No, I'm sure she'll survive.

JEFF. *(stops dead)* Wait! No one move! *(pats his shirt and pants pockets in a panic)* My keys! Who's got my keys! *(finds keys in pants pocket)* Oh. I've got my keys. False alarm.

(**JEFF** *and* **HARRIET** *exit to the trailer as* **VONDO** *enters from the theatre. NOTE:* **DANIEL**'s *responses to* **VONDO** *should be quick after every one of* **VONDO**'s *lines.*)

VONDO. Oh man, I love this show! *(goes to the van)* Hey Daniel, you're really good in the kick line.

(**DANIEL** *mimes a "thank you" bow.*)

Yeah, I'm having a good time. It's kinda like when we did Guys and… *(stops dead at the back of the van)* Where's my cooler?

(**DANIEL** *shivers.* **VONDO**, *trying to stay calm, walks around the van. To* **DANIEL** *with urgency in his voice.*)

Did you see my cooler?

(**DANIEL** *nods "yes" and shivers.*)

VONDO. *(cont.)* My Yoo-hoo is in that cooler.

(**DANIEL** *mimes drinking, then he rubs his tummy to mime "yummy".*)

Daniel! This is serious.

(**DANIEL** *makes a very serious face.*)

Tell me where my cooler is.

(**DANIEL** *mimes "no".*)

I need my cooler Goddamn it!

(**DANIEL** *makes the sign of the cross.*)

WHY ARE YOU DOING THIS!

(**DANIEL** *mimes "why".*)

WHY?

(**DANIEL** *mimes "why".*)

WHY!?!?

(**DANIEL** *mimes "why".*)

I *NEED* MY COOLER! DO YOU UNDERSTAND?

(**DANIEL** *nods "yes".*)

DON'T JUST LOOK AT ME!

(**DANIEL** *puts both hands to his eye like binoculars.* **VONDO** *grabs* **DANIEL** *by the shoulders.*)

STOP LOOKING AT ME!

(**DANIEL** *puts his hands over his eyes.* **VONDO** *throws* **DANIEL** *on the ground. Sits on him.*)

WHERE'S MY COOLER!

(**VONDO** *begins choking him.*)

TELL ME YOU MIMIN' MOTHER FUCKER! WHO'S GOT MY YOO-HOO?!

(**MIKE** *opens stage door, sees* **VONDO**, *runs over and tries to pull him off* **DANIEL**.)

MIKE. VONDO!

VONDO. *(as he continues to choke* **DANIEL***)* SPEAK! SPEAK! WHERE'S MY COOLER?

MIKE. *(Pulls* **VONDO** *off* **DANIEL***.)* I TOOK IT! It's onstage!

*(***VONDO** *bolts in the theatre. To* **DANIEL***.)*

Are you okay?

DANIEL. He assaulted me! I might sue him! You're a witness! I might sue him!

MIKE. Calm down!

DANIEL. No! I'll hire Robin's father and I'll sue him!

MIKE. That's what you get. You carried this mime thing too far.

DANIEL. I was enhancing my art!

MIKE. Oh come on, you provoked him. You provoke everybody to the point of hostility.

DANIEL. That's a lie! Everyone at this theatre loves me.

*(***JEANNIE** *opens the stage door and looks out with a big smile on her face. Sees* **DANIEL***, her smile fades.)*

JEANNIE. *(calling with disgust into the theatre)* He's still alive.

(An audible groan is heard inside as **JEANNIE** *exits.)*

*(***VONDO** *enters as calm as can be. He is holding a can or bottle of Yoo-hoo.)*

VONDO. *(with a smile, to* **DANIEL***)* Hey, I get it. That shivering thing, meant my cooler, right? Pretty clever. *(sits on the back of his van)*

*(***SCOTT** *enters running with a big smile and exits running into the theatre.)*

DANIEL. *(crosses to* **MIKE***)* I don't care what you say. I might sue him! *(exits in a snit to the theatre)*

MIKE. *(sits next to* **VONDO** *and looks at him a moment)* You okay?

VONDO. *(as if nothing happened)* Yeah. *(sips his Yoo-hoo)*

MIKE. Okay.

(**SCOTT** *enters, dragging* **JEANNIE** *by the hand out of the theatre*)

JEANNIE. What!

SCOTT. *(looks* **JEANNIE** *in the eye and says very definitely)* Caligula!

JEANNIE. Seriously?

SCOTT. *(reads quickly off his smartphone)* Born in 12 A.D., Caligula was a cruel, murderous emperor who engaged in homosexual sex with many men including a celebrated Greek actor, *(looks at everyone)* wow, big surprised there, *(reading)* as well as his brother in-law, Marcus Aemilius Lepidus!

JEANNIE. You can't use him. He's not even from this millennium.

SCOTT. *(points to* **VONDO***)* Can I get a ruling from the judges?

VONDO. *(gives two thumbs up; makes game show bell sound)* Ding, ding, ding!

SCOTT. *(to* **JEANNIE***)* AND YOU ARE OUTTA HERE! *(à la evangelical preacher out to the audience as if they were his congregation)* Yea, it was a dark time for us brethren. But now, in the throes of our oppression, we have been set free. Free to journey down the straight and narrow path – well, maybe just the narrow path, never again to be affiliated with, the party of the first part, now and forever to be known as, Daniel – the idiot straight guy, *(really rubs it in)* who's also a mime. HALLELUJAH, COME ON GET HAPPY, FOR THE FAT LADY HAS SUNG! *(Without getting too ridiculous or over the top,* **SCOTT** *does a celebratory dance more: either the hip-hop head snake move, or a toned down running man/Roger Rabbit.)*

MIKE. *(annoyed, opens the stage door and points for them to get inside)* Can we please finish this show!

VONDO. *(to* **MIKE***)* Whoa bro, stop and smell the roses. *(puts his arm around* **SCOTT***)* Six weeks ago this man could barely say the word gay, and today *(getting choked up)*

– he's led his people to the Promised Land. *(Sings, holding back the tears. To* **SCOTT***.)* This land is your land, this land is my land, *(looks front)* from San Francisco, to Fire Island

(as he and **SCOTT** *exit into the theatre)*

…la, la, la, la, la…la, la, la, la, la…

JEANNIE. *(stops at the door, looks to* **MIKE***)* Caligula.

*(***MIKE** *points for her to get in* **JEANNIE** *and* **MIKE** *exit into the theatre, lights dim,* This Land is Your Land, *plays.)*

Scene II

(Music changes to a melancholy tune. Lights come up. The marquee is changed and reads: "Now Playing – Glass Menagerie". The added sign reads: "Jack And The Beanstalk". There are two racks with costumes hung on them. One rack's sign reads: "Menagerie". The other reads: "Jack". JEANNIE's legs are hanging out from the van. She will remain asleep. It's opening night, 10 minutes before curtain. VONDO, JEFF and MEREDITH are sitting on the ground in front of the van. VONDO is eating Cheetos. MEREDITH is not in a costume.)

MEREDITH. *(depressed)* So the show has a helicopter. Our stage is big, we could land a helicopter. Oh come on, Miss Saigon is such a beautiful story. An innocent girl gives her heart to the man she loves, he uses her, rejects her, destroys her soul. I can play Asian. Or what about Les Mis, oh God, I'd kill to do that role. An innocent girl gives her heart to the man she loves, he uses her, abandons her, leaves her to starve in the street. *(looks at VONDO)* I can play famished.

VONDO. *(offers bag to MEREDITH)* Cheeto?

MEREDITH. *(shakes her head no, looks at JEFF)* We broke up.

JEFF. Yeah, I know.

MEREDITH. How'd you find out?

JEFF. Daniel mimed it to me.

MEREDITH. I can't believe he didn't give me that part. Goddamn him! He treated me like everyone who auditioned. Well, I'm not typical. I'll never end up being someone like, ya know, *(looks to make sure no one else is around)* Harriet. Don't get me wrong, she's a very nice person, but the thought of living her little housewife life makes my skin crawl. Oooh, let's go to pasta night at the Olive Garden before we go to bingo. That'll never be me. I want more. I want to be the woman that haunts men in theirs dreams. You know, like in *Fatal Attraction.* Now that would make a great show. An innocent woman gives her heart to a man she loves, he uses her, dumps hers, makes her an unstable, revenge seeking manic. Very relatable. *(turns to* **JEFF***)* I can play a stalker.

JEFF. *(beat)* This is one time I'll agree with you.

(**MIKE** *enters,* **DANIEL** *follows dragging* **ROBIN** *by the hand. He's playing the Gentleman Caller but isn't in costume. He wears black dance shorts and a black tee shirt that says: Mime! The Musical in white.* **ROBIN** *is playing Laura and wears a dull colored dress.)*

DANIEL. Mike! Mike! Mike!

VONDO. Hey, he's talkin' again. *(offers bag to* **DANIEL***)* Cheeto?

DANIEL. Don't ignore me! It'll give the gentleman caller diversity!

MIKE. The script says you do a few, emphasis on the word few, steps with her. Then you turn her, she knocks over her unicorn, it shatters, so does her life – end of dancing.

DANIEL. How 'bout I make them a few tap steps to lighten things up? This show's too dark!

MIKE. I know you were at rehearsals, I saw you there. For the last time, her character is crippled. She hobbles around the whole show!

ROBIN. Besides, how do you tap dance with a limp?

DANIEL. Duh! You wouldn't be tap dancing. I'd be tap dancing. *(he taps around* **ROBIN***)* You'd just try a step and I'll spin you around with a strength move *(spins* **ROBIN***)* and then you'll break the horsey.

MIKE. LAURA DOES NOT TAP DANCE! SHE'S LAME!

JEFF. *(to* **MIKE***)* She's not the only one.

MIKE. Listen, this is one of the Tennessee Williams' greatest works and you're not going to screw with it.

(**HARRIET** *enters. She's playing Amanda and is dressed in a drab dress.)*

DANIEL. Oh yeah, well if it's so great why didn't they make it into a musical, huh? Could the reason be, I dunno… it's too dark. *(sees* **HARRIET***)* Oh! How about if I dance with Harriet?

MIKE. NO!

DANIEL. Well you can't stop me once I'm onstage.

HARRIET. *(sweetly)* Daniel dear, make no mistake – you dance with me and I'll take every pair of tap shoes you own and shove them up your ass.

ROBIN. Daniel, why do you always to this? Why do you always try to change everything right before curtain? You make me so nervous I have to pee! *(exits into the theatre)*

DANIEL. See? That's good. She's supposed to be nervous. Having to pee will enhance her character. Well, I don't care what anyone says, my way is better! I bet if Tennessee Williams was here he'd think so too.

MIKE. *(annoyed, trying to get rid of him)* Shouldn't you be in costume?

DANIEL. I don't come on until scene six.

VONDO. What's with the mime shirt?

DANIEL. It's my marketing strategy. I wear this shirt and everywhere I go people just stare at me and say, "Who would do a musical about mimes?" See? They're intrigued with the idea! *(to* **MIKE***)* Did Aunt Phyllis call you? *(looks at* **JEFF***)* She said I could call her Aunt Phyllis, ya know.

MIKE. Yeah, she called.

DANIEL. She wants to have me and Eric at the board meeting to talk about the show, right?

MIKE. Yeah.

DANIEL. Yes! She wants you to produce it, ya know. She really loves it. And you better listen to her cause you're on thin ice right now. Ya see, people like uplifting stuff – stuff that can be turned into a musical. That's the problem with this show. No place for a tap number, no place for a kick line. *(as he exits into the theatre)* It's too dark! *(exits)*

JEFF. *(to MIKE)* Are you out of your freakin' mind? You're meeting with Phyllis about his play?

MIKE. Hey, don't give me crap. This is all your fault. You're the one who said we'd consider it.

JEFF. Yeah well, that was different, I was lying.

MIKE. Look – she's all ready threatened to pull the money. She's talked the board into making Eric literary manager to "help me" pick next season. And she's in my face every time I turn around, so gimme a break, will ya?

JEFF. I told you, don't get them involved with picking the shows. You saw what happened, they'll ruin this place.

MIKE. *(snaps)* I know!

JEFF. Well then don't let them think you're giving in!

(JEFF *crosses to* VONDO *and* HARRIET. *Trying to break the tension,* VONDO *holds out bag of Cheetos to* JEFF.)

VONDO. Cheeto?

JEFF. Don't eat too many of those. I've got tons of food back at my house.

HARRIET. Oh I'm sorry, didn't Scott tell you? I can't make the party tonight. I've got a date with my husband.

MEREDITH. Oh isn't that cute… *(looks at* JEFF *and* VONDO *and says condescendingly)* she dates her husband.

HARRIET. Well, that's what he likes to call it. It's sort of our anniversary. We were married on the 24th and every month on that date he plans something special. Tonight we're going on a midnight dinner cruise.

MEREDITH. Oh isn't it nice you two go out to dinner once a month.

HARRIET. Well, we just don't go out to dinner, dear. Bill finds all kinds of ways to do special things for me on that day. Once, we were walking in the park and he had a surprise picnic lunch waiting there.

(Unimpressed, **MEREDITH** *makes a* subtle *expression or gesture to condescendingly indicate "oooh, big whoop" to herself.)*

HARRIET. *(a little flustered)* Oh, and then there was this one time, oh my, he did the most unbelievable thing – with roses.

MEREDITH. *(Slowly turns and looks at* **HARRIET.** *Quietly.)* Roses?

HARRIET. Uh-huh. Total strangers came up to me all day and handed me roses. I went to the cleaners, I got a rose. I went to the gas station, I got a rose. I went to pay the taxes, I got a rose. I don't know how he did it. Oh and this is good, last month we got in the car and I thought we were going to buy a storm door for our mudroom. The next thing I knew we were on the ferry to Nantucket. If you ever go, you have to stay at the Bed and Breakfast we stayed at.

MEREDITH. Is it on the ocean?

HARRIET. Uh-huh. Oh, and you'll love this, Bill borrowed that lace dress I wore in *Ragtime* and had it there in the room with a straw hat and a vest for him. Well, we got dressed, went outside, and there was a bicycle built for two leaning against a tree. So, we pedaled to this little ice cream parlor and you know what he did next?

MEREDITH. *(almost afraid to ask)* What?

HARRIET. There was a player piano there and he put a quarter in it and sang *Let Me Call You Sweetheart,* right there in front of everyone. I was blushing from head to toe. I have to hand it to him – he's certainly creative. In thirty-nine years he's never done the same thing twice.

MEREDITH. He's done this for thirty-nine years?

HARRIET. Uh, huh. Oh, but he really got me good once. It was almost midnight on the 24th and nothing had happened all day. So we go to bed, Bill kisses me goodnight, turns out the light and I thought, oh my goodness, he forgot. Then all of a sudden, a mariachi band starts serenading us under our window. *(laughs a little at herself)* Oh, I'm sorry, I know I go on. But I can't help it. After all these years, he still makes me feel like we're on our honeymoon.

MEREDITH. *(Looks at* **HARRIET**. *Beat.)* My life sucks. *(sobs)* MY LIFE SUCKS SO MUCH I CAN'T STAND IT! Nothing like that ever happens to me and it should. *(to* **VONDO**) I work at the mall. How sucky is that?

VONDO. *(unsure of how to calm her, holds up the bag of Cheetos to* **MEREDITH**) Cheeto?

MEREDITH. Oh God, my life sucks!

*(**MEREDITH** exits running around the back of the theatre as **ERIC** enters passing her.)*

MIKE. *(starts after her, stops)* I can't do this again. *(to* **VONDO**) Will you go talk to her?

VONDO. Okay. *(gets up, puts down bag)* Ya know, this is interesting. I've never been around Meredith when she wasn't playing a character. *(exits after* **MEREDITH** *with the bag of Cheetos)*

HARRIET. You know he's right. This is the first time I've ever seen Meredith's real personality emerge too. Poor thing, I think I like her better as Medea.

ERIC. *(enters from the theatre)* Michael, I want to see your choices for next season as soon a possible.

MIKE. Look, I just had Daniel harassing me. I don't need you breathing down my neck too.

ERIC. Peasant! Don't dismiss me.

HARRIET. Eric, why don't you talk about this after the show?

ERIC. *(with a southern accent)* Mother! Why do you persecute me? Set me free, damn you! Set me free!

HARRIET. *(to* **JEFF** *who looks puzzled)* He likes to be in character when he talks to me. I don't mind it so much when we're here, but he caused quite a commotion when I saw him at Sears.

ERIC. *(hands* **MIKE** *a piece of paper)* Here are the shows I want to do and Aunt Phyllis will have hers when we meet tomorrow.

MIKE. *(Feels* **JEFF** *glaring at him. To* **JEFF.***)* I'm just gonna listen to their ideas, okay? I have to listen to them to some extent, don't I?

ERIC. If you're smart you'll do more than just listen.

*(***MEREDITH*** and* ***VONDO*** enter.* ***MEREDITH*** has the cell phone, listening to* ***REBA.****)*

MIKE. Shut up. *(to* **JEFF** *trying to be diplomatic)* Look, I know you're not going to want to hear this, but Phyllis does have a valid point. If she's going to give us all this money, she should at least be able to sit down with me and…

JEFF. No, no, sit down with her. Get cozy, be chums. I think it's great. But when this place shuts down because we don't have an audience, don't say I didn't warn you. You're sure making me feel like I made the right decision.

HARRIET. *(trying to avoid unpleasantness)* You know, I think it's time we all go in.

ERIC. *(in a southern accent as Tom)* Why do you smother me, Mother! Give me air! I need air!

(as **HARRIET**, **JEFF** *and* **ERIC** *walk to the theatre door)*

HARRIET. *(to* **JEFF***)* Performing in the theatre is one of the most rewarding experiences you can have, right?

JEFF. Yeah.

HARRIET. Just checkin'.

*(***HARRIET*** and* ***JEFF*** exit into the theatre.)*

ERIC. *(calls after them)* Go ahead and mock me! *(turns back to* **MIKE***)* I am *persona non grata*! *(exits)*

MEREDITH. *(depressed, to* **REBA***)* Okay. Yeah, I'll try. Thanks. *(hands phone to* **VONDO**, *looks at* **MIKE***)*

VONDO. *(to* REBA*)* So, how'd ya do? Yeah, tell me about it, I get to go to the cast party and hear it all over again.

(Stands there looking at MIKE *and* MEREDITH. *Silence.)*

Nope. They're not talking. *(sits, looks at them)* Nope. They're just lookin' at each other.

*(*MIKE *and* MEREDITH *look at* VONDO.*)*

VONDO. Now they're lookin' at me. *(beat)* What? *(beat)* OH! *(quickly stands, to* MIKE *and* MEREDITH*)* Ah…I gotta go in and *(thinks hard, points to phone)* …get Reba more Cheetos. Bye. *(exits)*

MIKE. As you can see, things aren't really going well right now. So can you cut me a break and stop?

(silence from MEREDITH*)*

Look, whether you want to admit it or not, Robin's good.

MEREDITH. Oh, she's Robin for this show? You mean she didn't change her name to "Penny Sillin?"

MIKE. Don't pick on her. She's a sweet kid, she's worked hard and she's damn good in the role. Look, I did what's best for the show, not for you. So will you just cut it out; I've got enough problems.

MEREDITH. I never wanted to be a problem. *(sincerely)* I just wanted to be with you.

*(*MIKE *turns and looks at her, but she just can't let it go.)*

AND I WANTED THAT PART! I thought you cared!

MIKE. I do! But I gave the role to Robin because she's better suited than you.

MEREDITH. Are you kidding me? She's better suited for Laura then me? Oh God, and I wore stilettos and a thong for you. Laura is a desolate, lonely character. What makes you think Robin has a clue how to play her? She's pretty, she's talented, *everybody* loves her. And – she's got a rich daddy who's gonna hand her a perfect world on a silver platter. Oh yeah, I see the similarities. I can't believe Jeff's going to let you run this place! You're screwing it up already! Eric's right, you're pathetic and everyone knows it!

MIKE. *(That's it. He's lost it.)* Okay, ya really want to know why you didn't get the part? I didn't want to embarrass you. Stand in front of the mirror and take a good look at yourself because it's pretty obvious. You can't play Laura and the audience would think the same thing the second they'd see you! The truth is you didn't get the part because you're too Goddamn... *(he can't do it)* tall.

MEREDITH. *(looks at him a moment)* I can play short.

MIKE. *(snaps)* Stop it!

MEREDITH. *(almost in tears)* I'm sorry. Not getting this part made me feel so rejected. This is the only place in the world I've ever felt important. I can demand respect here.

MIKE. You can demand it all you want, but you'll never have it till you earn it. Do you think being difficult gives you credibility as an actress – cause it doesn't. I'm sick of trying to defend you to everyone. And you get worse every show.

MEREDITH. *(quietly)* Well I can't help it. I'm a diva.

MIKE. No – Maria Callas was a diva. You drive a Volkswagen.

MEREDITH. *(this is really hard for her)* Look, *(beat)* I don't have a life, okay? I'm a replaceable nobody at a nothing job. What few friends I have are married. I get to watch them plan their futures, when most of my year is spent counting the days until this place opens. I love it here. That's why when I get a part it's all I can think about. Come on Mike, you know I really do work hard. And nobody sees it. No one appreciates me.

MIKE. What do you want them to do, thank you every time you berate them? People aren't here to fill a tremendous void in your life. They're doing it because they love theatre just as much as you do. And there's nothing wrong with trying to be nice. Did you ever stop to think it might even help your performance?

For one, it might get Jeannie to quit filling your shoes with Cheese Whiz every time you have a quick change.

MEREDITH. See, that's exactly what I mean. She doesn't take her work seriously!

MIKE. No – she doesn't take *your* work seriously. And who can blame her, you're unbearable. So unbearable that people are forgetting you have talent. Look, let's just forget about it for now, okay?

MEREDITH. You think you might want to give us another chance?

MIKE. We better give that a break too.

MEREDITH. Oh God, I'm such a loser.

MIKE. *(sympathetically)* Come on, don't do this. Face it, we're not meant for each other. You're a person who lives for the theatre, who's very intense about acting methods and performing – and I'm a person who's... normal. I gotta go in. Wanna come?

MEREDITH. I guess.

MIKE. Let me give you some advice. Just calm down. If you keep having all these outrageous expectations of people, you're never gonna be happy. You're a nice person, but no one knows it. Okay?

MEREDITH. I want a mariachi band.

MIKE. What about Vondo playing "Smoke On The Water" in a sombrero?

MEREDITH. *(Defeated, she smiles with tears in her eyes.)* I'll take it.

(**MIKE** *smiles, gives her a kiss on her head. He puts his arm around her and they walk toward the theatre door.* **SCOTT** *enters from the theatre.*)

SCOTT. *(to* **MIKE***)* Where's Jeannie?

(**MIKE** *points to the van.* **SCOTT** *walks to the van as* **MIKE** *and* **MEREDITH** *exit into the theatre.*)

Jeannie! They're calling places.

(There is no response. **SCOTT** *bangs side of the van.)*

JEANNIE!!

JEANNIE. *(sits up abruptly, barely awake and panicked)* RIGHT! I'M GOOD! HI!

SCOTT. Come on, sunshine, let's move it.

JEANNIE. *(takes a breath)* Okay. Ah, what show are we doing?

SCOTT. *Glass Menagerie.*

JEANNIE. *Glass Menagerie* – which one?

SCOTT. What are you talking about? *(grabs a vest from rack)*

JEANNIE. *(as she gets costume pieces from rack)* Oh God, I am losing it. I dreamt Daniel was in a hysterical panic because the show just got turned into a musical and we had to change all the blocking before 8 o'clock. So I ran to the office to get a pencil and Tennessee Williams was there yelling at Mike because there weren't any kick lines. *(beat)* Plus he wanted Asians and a helicopter. And the whole time this was going on, Vondo was just standing there playing "Smoke on the Water". But for some reason, he was only wearing stilettos and a thong.

SCOTT. *(stares at her in disbelief)* Wow. We better get you a cup of coffee, quick.

JEANNIE. *(walks to the theatre)* No, actually I have this incredible craving for Cheetos – and I don't know why.

*(***SCOTT*** *and* ***JEANNIE*** *exit in to the theatre, lights dim as music to* West Side Story *fades in.)*

Scene III

(Lights up. Time: opening night, near the end of Act I. Marquee reads: "West Side Story". The added sign reads: "Children's Theatre Now Presenting: Sleeping Beauty". Again, two costume racks with signs – one on the right of the stage door reads: "West Side", the other on the left reads: "Beauty". HARRIET is repairing a costume. JEANNIE is lying down, legs dangle out the back of the van, SCOTT is sitting next to her. They're both completely exhausted.)

HARRIET. Five performances of Sleeping Beauty?! Dear Lord, how did you manage it?

SCOTT. *(with his eyes closed)* It wouldn't have been so bad, but Vondo plays the King and a guard. We had to keep changing him back and forth and back and forth.

JEANNIE. I've changed Vondo's clothes twenty-seven times today. *(sits up)* And in two minutes, I get to peel yet another sweat soaked costume and change him from Glad Hand into a Jet. Has Mike said anything to you about this afternoon?

HARRIET. No. Why? What happened?

SCOTT. Oh Jesus – World War III! They had that board meeting. Everyone said they were screaming. Mike stormed out twice. Diane Perry said when he came back the second time, he had a lawyer with him. We don't know what the hell's going on.

JEANNIE. Jeff's really worried about him.

(ROBIN enters. She is playing Maria and wears a white dress with a red sash. If her hair is not dark, she wears a dark wig. Her expression looks like she has just eaten something bad. She walks over to the prop table where she has a bottle of water.)

HARRIET. What's the matter Robin?

ROBIN. I don't like kissing Daniel. I know my character's supposed to be in love with him, but I can't help it. He smells like pepperoni. *(takes a small sip of water)*

JEANNIE. Oh God help me. I'm so tired I can't even reply to that. *(leans on the van with her eyes closed)*

HARRIET. *(to* **ROBIN***)* Honey, do you need some help with your change?

ROBIN. *(a little gargle with the water, then swallows)* Thanks, but I think I want to watch the rumble first. That's my second favorite scene. My first favorite scene is "America". I love that! What's your favorite scene, Jeannie?

JEANNIE. Eric getting stabbed or Daniel getting shot. *(lays down)*

ROBIN. Know what? Mike picked next season. But he's not telling anyone yet. Daniel's going nuts. He keeps bugging him and bugging him. Jeff told Daniel if he asks Mike one more time, he was gonna put real bullets in Chino's gun. The only thing announced is Sue Logan is in charge of children's programming. I'm gonna go watch. *(exits into the theatre passing* **VONDO***)*

*(***VONDO*** enters dressed as Glad Hand. He quickly takes off his jacket, shirt and hat. NOTE: The last thing he does is take his phone out of his pocket and will hold it in his hand while* **JEANNIE** *and* **SCOTT** *change him. Make sure that the King's costume, whether a robe, tunic, etc., is loose fitting, or designed so it can be put on VONDO easily. During the next exchange,* **JEANNIE** *and* **SCOTT** *are so tired, they become a little giggly and punch drunk and don't pay attention to what they are doing.)*

HARRIET. Well duty calls. Hang in there guys, the day is almost over. *(exits to the trailer)*

SCOTT. Looks like the children's theatre is staying. *(begins to change* **VONDO***)*

(Hands **SCOTT** *robe.* **SCOTT** *begins dressing* **VONDO** *as the King.)*

JEANNIE. Yeah, well, Sue's a good choice. At least he didn't give the job to Eric. *(giggling)* Could you imagine him directing the kid's shows? Snow White And The Seven Serial Killers. We would have Dopey, Gacey, Bundy, Dahmer.

(hands SCOTT *cape)*

No wait! Even better – Nightmare on Sesame Street.

(They go into hysterics.)

SCOTT. *(as he puts a cape on* VONDO*)* Stop.

JEANNIE. *(hands* SCOTT *crown)* Aw, come on. Wouldn't you pay to see Elmo hacking the hell outta Bert and Ernie? I know I would. Screw *Peter Pan,* cut me up a Muppet, now that's entertainment. *(cracking herself up,* JEANNIE *hands* VONDO *his scepter)*

SCOTT. You are so going to hell.

*(*JEANNIE *and* SCOTT *laughing, stroll to the van and lie down as* VONDO *gets a call.)*

VONDO. Oh! I'm buzzin'! *(answers phone)* Hey Babe, can't talk, I'm going on. No, I got an extra part. *(as he exits into the theatre)* I'm in the rumble, I'm playing a Jet. *(exits)*

(Silence. A few beats go by…)

JEANNIE. Scott? Did he say he was playing a Jet?

SCOTT. *(beat)* SHIT!

(They both spring up and bolt for the stage door.)

MIKE. *(enters, shaking his head and smiling)* That's one weird looking rumble.

JEANNIE. Oh God! We didn't do this! Tell me we didn't do this.

MIKE. What happened?

SCOTT. I don't know. We weren't thinking, we're burned out, goddamn it!

MEREDITH. *(Enters laughing. She's playing Anita and wears a mambo dress. If her hair is not dark, she wears a dark wig.)* I don't know what happened. I don't care. It's just nice for once it didn't happen to me.

MIKE. Is Jeff upset?

MEREDITH. Oh, I think stunned is more the word. Actually it's quite entertaining watching Vondo fend off a switchblade with a scepter.

MIKE. Oh God, he's gonna kill me. *(exits in the theatre)*

MEREDITH. *(scolding)* What is wrong with you guys? Stupid mistakes like that could ruin a whole season.

SCOTT. *(snaps)* Look, we screwed up, okay? Not that you care because it's not about you, but we're working our asses off–we're having a hard time handling things– and yes–we made a mistake. But hey, thanks for kicking us while we're down.

MEREDITH. *(starts walking off, stops, and then, not overly enthusiastically)* You know, if things are really that bad, I'll come in and help.

SCOTT. *(turns and looks at **MEREDITH**)* Help who?

MEREDITH. Help you.

JEANNIE. *(uneasily)* Do what?

MEREDITH. Whatever you need. Just let me know. *(exits to the costume trailer)*

SCOTT. *(looks at **JEANNIE**)* What the hell was that?

JEANNIE. I don't know. But it made the hair on my arms stand up. *(rubs her arm)*

*(**VONDO** opens the stage door to enter. As he does we hear **DANIEL**, off-stage, as Tony.)*

DANIEL. *(cries out and will continue until **JEFF** slams the door)* MARIAAAAA!!!!!!!

*(The following happens at a quick pace. As **DANIEL** cries out, **VONDO** crosses to cooler for a Yoo-hoo. As he crosses, **ROBIN** enters, runs over to the costume rack, grabs her dress for the next scene and quickly exits to the trailer. As she exits, **JEFF** enters and slams the door.)*

JEFF. *(walking slowly center)* Okay kiddies, time for a chat. It has come to my attention this evening that we're not all doing the same show here. Now look, I know you're both really beat, but for the remainder of the evening, can we keep our characters straight? We're doing *West Side Story*. At the end of the show Tony is shot by Chino – not Rumplestilskin. Okay? Okay. *(says his speech abridged)* Oh yeah, by the way, ya know, great, proud, teamwork, motto, show.

*(**VONDO** gives him a thumbs up.)*

*(**SCOTT** takes **VONDO**'s crown, etc., hangs them up. **DANIEL** enters and is dressed as Tony. He has a big smile and looks very excited.)*

DANIEL. Well, well, well...I hope egg is in style, because you're all going to be wearing it on your faces. Guess what? *(beat and then he blurts out:)* Mike folded, Eric won. We're doing my musical next season!

JEANNIE. Yeah right.

DANIEL. It's true! *(to JEFF)* Mike left his notebook in the office. After everyone left the board meeting I snuck in there and looked. I knew you wouldn't believe me, so I photocopied it. *(hands JEFF the paper)* It's right there in Mike's own handwriting.

JEFF. *(looks at paper.)* Holy shit. It's there. *(looks at them amazed)* I'm not kidding. It's really there.

SCOTT. No way!

JEANNIE. Gimme that! *(looks at paper)* Oh my God, the letters are on the page and they really form the word.

DANIEL. See! Told you! We're even going to close the season with it!

JEFF. That's got to be a mistake.

DANIEL. You'd like to think that, wouldn't ya? But it's not. I heard that Aunt Phyllis was yelling at him in his office today. She must've put him in his place! I bet you guys are feeling pretty stupid.

SCOTT. Oh shut up and go get changed.

DANIEL. Oh yeah, well you shut up! Shut up yourself! Soon, all you're gonna see are posters around here that say, The Neighborhood Actors Summerfun Repertory Theatre proudly presents, Mime! – The Musical! Next season Eric will have creative control and he'll be calling the shots. And he likes me. So think twice before you pick on me again! My talent has finally been recognized! I am no longer – PERSONA...AU GRATIN!

(**DANIEL** *and* **SCOTT** *exit into the theatre.*)

JEFF. I can't believe this. For twelve years I've done everything I could, even tapping into my retirement to keep this theatre going. Then I hand it over to the one person I thought I could trust, and the bastard sells me out.

(**MEREDITH** *and* **HARRIET** *enter.* **MEREDITH** *is dressed for Act II and is looking at pictures on* **HARRIET**'s *phone.*)

MEREDITH. Wow. These really came out good.

JEFF. *Oklahoma* pictures?

HARRIET. Uh-huh. *(to* **MEREDITH***)* Oh, there might be a few family shots mixed in there.

MEREDITH. Nice picture of you and Bill. *(goes to the next picture)* Whoa – who's the hunk?

HARRIET. Oh that's my son, Kurt.

MEREDITH. You have a son? *(looks at the picture)* Oh my God, he's gorgeous. *(swipes the phone screen quickly to look at the rest of the pictures)* Gee, I don't see any pictures of his wife.

HARRIET. He's not married.

MEREDITH. Why, what's wrong with him? *(quickly catches herself)* I mean, why not?

HARRIET. He had a fiancée but she was a real corporate go-getter. Between his job and hers, they never saw each other.

MEREDITH. What does he do?

HARRIET. He's an archeologist.

MEREDITH. *(enamored)* Oh my God, you mean, like Harrison Ford in *Raiders Of The Lost Ark*?

HARRIET. Well, I guess. Right now he's just finishing a project in Casablanca.

MEREDITH. *(a little stunned)* Casablanca? Are you kidding me? People really go there? That is so cool. *(She likes saying the word.)* He's in…Casa-blan-ca.

HARRIET. Well he's not there long, he'll be home Monday.

MEREDITH. Oh! Well tell him to see the show! I'd love to meet him.

HARRIET. *(very reluctant)* Oh. Oh, honey…oh, God no. I mean, I really don't think he's your type.

MEREDITH. No no, that doesn't matter anymore. Mike and I had a talk and ever since, I've been looking at things a little differently. Oh my God, Harriet! I've just got to meet him, okay? How about if you and I go out after the show! Then you can tell me all about him! Won't that be fun? Great! I'm gonna friend him on Facebook.

(Startles HARRIET by giving her a hug, and exits to the trailer.)

HARRIET. Well, it looks like I've acquired a new friend. I just want you all to know–he's going to hate her. He's going to absolutely hate her. Then he's going to hate me, then I'm going to hate Mike. It's a vicious circle. I don't know what Mike said to her, but I mean it – I liked her better as Medea. *(exits into the theatre)*

ERIC. *(Enters bolting out of the theatre. He's playing Bernardo.)* Have you heard? Not only has Mike chosen to do our musical, he's making it the season finale! Finally, there's someone at the helm that won't suppress me. Oh! My mind is wild with character concepts. *(gasps)* There can be a codependent mime, a suicidal mime, an abused mime.

JEANNIE. If you do this show, they'll all be abused mimes.

ERIC. Why do I try to impress the minions? This will be astounding! I gotta make notes! *(Runs for the theatre door and stops. To* **JEFF**.*)* Thank God you're gone. *(exits into the theatre)*

JEANNIE. I'll quit. I swear to God, I'll quit. *(***JEANNIE** *folds her arms, turns her back to the audience.)*

VONDO. Man, what am I gonna do if I don't come here? I gotta be in some kind of group. I can't get classified as a loner – people get nervous enough when I walk in the post office.

JEFF. Well, look at it this way, every end is a new beginning. I'm sure there's lots of other stuff you guys can… *(looks at* **JEANNIE** *a moment)* Are you crying?

JEANNIE. *(Turns her head slightly away from* **JEFF**. *She will not let anyone, audience included, see her cry.)* No.

JEFF. *(walks closer to her)* That's a tear.

JEANNIE. *(quickly wipes tear from her eye)* Shut up.

JEFF. *(smiles and almost touched)* Man, I figure you'd be the last person to have a soft spot for this place.

JEANNIE. Oh please – I'll be fine next summer doing nothing on the beach, thank you.

VONDO. *(stares out and then very thoughtfully)* Maybe I'll raise ferrets.

MIKE. *(enters)* Ten to places.

(The three glare at him.)

Something wrong?

(silence)

MIKE. *(cont.)*What's the matter?

*(***JEFF** *hands* **MIKE** *the piece of paper.* **MIKE** *looks at it.)*

Where did you get this?

JEFF. Daniel. He went through your notebook and made of copy of it.

MIKE. *(annoyed)* Oh Goddamn him. Well, I'm sorry. I was gonna tell you guys first before I announced it, but...I guess you know.

JEFF. That's it? Who the hell are you? Not only are you producing shit next season, you made shit the season finale! If I knew you were gonna do this, I would've saved myself some trouble and given the position to Eric. God Mike, I trusted you. And worse, considered you a friend. Now you're gonna take twelve years of my work and flush it down the toilet.

MIKE. Hey. Take it easy.

JEFF. Don't tell me to take it easy you ass-kissing wimp.

JEANNIE. Mike, I'm with Jeff. I'm not gonna bust my ass so you can ruin this theatre. I think I can speak for Vondo –

VONDO. *(states as fact)* I'm peeved.

JEANNIE. Don't expect us back.

MIKE. *(stunned)* Are you serious? *(beat)* Well, that's just fucking great. *(to JEFF)* You know, ever since you dumped this position on me, I've bent over backwards to keep peace despite everyone's threats and egos. *(to all three)* I figured if anyone would understand the crap I'm going through, you would. *(to JEFF)* So yeah, I didn't handle things your way, and I didn't pick the shows you'd pick. But I did what I had to do to make things work. And hey – I got the money. It doesn't matter if you don't like the way I got it. What matters is, I got it and we're gonna have another season. So if this is how you feel then go ahead and quit. I mean it, some fuckin' friends you turned out to be.

JEFF. Look who's talking. Just do me one favor – explain your logic! I wanna hear this. After all the years we've put into this place, you spineless son of a bitch, you at least owe us that.

MIKE. Fine! *(reads off the paper)* I picked *Gypsy* because that's a guaranteed money maker. We're doing *Camelot* cause the renaissance fair just gave us a ton of their old costumes. I think *The Odd Couple* explains itself as the comedy. I picked *The King And I,* because there's no way Daniel can tap dance in bare feet. *Mousetrap* is a mystery, that's different. And fuck you all, I'm closing the season with *Mame,* CAUSE GODDAMN IT, I LIKE *MAME.*

(JEANNIE, VONDO *and* JEFF *look at* MIKE.)

JEFF. *(looks at* JEANNIE*)* Oh Jesus…

VONDO. Mike…I'm gonna kiss you on the mouth.

MIKE. *(puzzled, then catches on)* Are you kidding me? Oh come on…what are you – on crack?

JEFF. Oh man, Mike, I'm sorry. I really am. I shoulda known better.

MIKE. Sorry my ass. That's what you think of me? Screw you.

(JEANNIE *takes out a small note pad and writes while walking over to* MIKE.)

JEFF. Hey, come on, in all fairness, *(points to the paper)* you gotta admit – that does look like Mime.

MIKE. Well yeah, I guess. But if you go by my handwriting, we're also doing Moosetrap and Cumalot.

JEANNIE. Michael, *(rips out paper from notebook, hands it to* MIKE*)* this is the name of my bank and the number of my safety deposit box. There you will find, the deed to my condo, the title to my car and various stocks and bonds. That's everything I own in the world. It's all yours – just let me tell them.

JEFF. Jeannie – I get Eric.

(He shakes hands with JEANNIE.*)*

MIKE. But guys, be gentle. I've got enough going on, I don't need them sobbing on my shoulder.

JEANNIE. Oh, don't worry. I know just how I'm gonna say it.

JEFF. So how the hell did you get Phyllis and the morons to see things your way?

MIKE. I didn't. Believe me, they were this close to kicking me out the door. Phyllis was adamant, she was not budging. So when we took a break, I left, did some begging and – I got Robin's dad to join the board. He walked in there, got them to listen and said he and his firm would gladly help fund the theatre provided his daughter wouldn't appear naked or bleeding again. You shoulda heard him, Jeff, it was a thing of beauty. Nothing like a good trial attorney to sway things in your favor.

JEFF. *(smiles at* MIKE *in amazement)* Well done, young Skywalker. *(pats him on the back)* Well done.

ERIC. *(enters quickly, now wearing a clean tee shirt)* Listen to this! I came up with the most beguiling idea! Heroin addicted runaways – who live on the streets as mimes! Just like *Rent*, but in whiteface.

JEFF. The last show of the season....is *Mame*.

ERIC. *Mame?*

JEANNIE. *Mame!* *(claps)*

ERIC. You're kidding, right? That's the season finale? That drivel is like the safest show in the world.

MIKE. Good. Then that's the one and only show you'll direct next year.

JEFF. THE ONE AND ONLY!

ERIC. Don't saddle me with this! How the hell will I make those characters controversial?

MIKE. You won't!

JEFF. HE WON'T!

(DANIEL *enters from the theatre.)*

JEFF. *(sees* DANIEL *and says joyfully)* DANIEL! Come on in here, buddy.

(DANIEL, *uncertain why* JEFF *is happy to see him, smiles anyway.* VONDO *sits on his cooler, polishing his guitar.* JEFF *leads* DANIEL *to* JEANNIE, *who begins to mime, "tying a knot".)*

ERIC. Peasant! I can't be pigeon-holed! I must create! All these one-dimensional characters do is sing and dance and drink martinis. *(beat)* Wait! Now, there's a point to explore –

MIKE. *(walks center and points finger at* **ERIC***)* Don't.

(This segment is three separate conversations. They switch from one actor to another and should be blocked so that the audience can easily follow them. They must flow quickly and smoothly. While the actors shouldn't rush their lines, they must not pause before saying their line because that it break the flow in the scene. There should no breaks of the action either. Also, during this exchange, a stage direction will have **JEFF** *handing* **MIKE** *the keys. This is a very important moment because* **JEFF** *is "passing the baton" and handing over the theatre to* **MIKE***. Make sure the two actors are blocked so the audience will clearly see* **JEFF** *handing the keys to* **MIKE***.)*

> **DANIEL.** What? You're tying something?

ERIC. Mame is perceived as this life loving, happy-go-lucky person.

> **(JEANNIE** *mimes pulling the ends of what she is tying harder, miming "tying a knot")*
> **DANIEL.** A bow? A knot?

(JEANNIE
*mimes on
the nosy,
mimes "I'm
in a box, I'm
pulling a
rope.")*

ERIC. But in
reality, she's a
child abusing
alcoholic!

MEREDITH. *(enters,
elated and
babbling.)*
GUESS WHAT!
Harriet's son
had all the leads
in his college
plays!

DANIEL. That's easy.
You're doing
mime.

(JEANNIE
*mimes
pulling a
knot again.)*

MEREDITH. He's
played Billy
Bigelow!

ERIC. We'll focus on
her battle with
the bottle.

MEREDITH. And Sky
Masterson!

DANIEL. Knot?
You're not
doing mime?

(JEANNIE
*smiles, nods
yes starts
pointing to*
DANIEL.)

MEREDITH. And
Henry Higgins!

DANIEL. I'm not
doing mime?
(JEANNIE
*smiles, does
"on the
nosy")*

MEREDITH. Harriet
said he's gonna
be home for at
least a year!

ERIC. Meredith can
go to an A.A.
meeting in
costume.

DANIEL. Sounds
like?
(JEANNIE
*drags her leg
like* ROBIN
in Glass
Menagerie.)

MEREDITH. *(runs
to* MIKE*)* Mike,
you gotta ask
him to audition.
Please!

ERIC. Hi, my name's
Mame and I'm
an alcoholic."

VONDO. *(not looking up from polishing his guitar)* Hi Mame.

JEFF. *(to* **ERIC***)* YOU are sick!

                         MEREDITH. *(to* **MIKE***)* You're in charge!

            DANIEL. You're confusing me!
            *(***JEANNIE** *drags her leg)*

ERIC. Discount tickets for recovering alcoholics!

            DANIEL. Limp?

*(***JEFF** *strolls center to* **MIKE***, takes his keys, puts his arm around* **MIKE***.* **JEFF** *smiles, holds up keys, drops them into* **MIKE***'s hand. He pats* **MIKE** *on the back, walks to the theatre door.* **MIKE** *walks to the van.)*

                         MEREDITH. Are there any musicals with like a Mexican theme?

            DANIEL. Lame? Sounds like lame?
              *(***JEANNIE** *pulls her ear)*

                         MEREDITH. Heck, we can write our own.

DANIEL. You're not
   performing
   mime…
   (concentrates)
   you're
   performing…

MEREDITH. *(gasps
   with excitement)*
   THE ALAMO!

DANIEL. *(thinks hard)*
   Fame!

*(VONDO gets
phone, makes
   a call)*

MEREDITH. Now
   there's a
   musical for you!

ERIC. Where's my
   notebook? *(takes
   notebook out of
   his backpack, sits
   by van, begins
   writing notes)*

DANIEL. Blame?

MEREDITH. I can
   play wounded.

DANIEL. Game?

VONDO. *(to REBA)*
   Hey, Baby!
   Good news
   – *Mame* not
   Mime.

(JEANNIE
gestures
largely with
both arms to
VONDO)

DANIEL. Tame?

ERIC. Mame will be
true...
Mame will be
real...

(JEANNIE
gestures
largely with
both arms to
ERIC)
DANIEL. Same?

ERIC. Mame will
bring me glory!

DANIEL. Do it again.
I know I can
get it!

(JEANNIE
stares at
DANIEL *in*
disbelief)

MEREDITH. Oh God,
I'm so happy!
I can't wait till
next year!

(JEANNIE *turns, walks towards the van.* **DANIEL** *follows*)

HARRIET. *(Opens door, stands in doorway.)* Five to places!

VONDO. I'll explain later.

ERIC. Opening night will be one big A.A. meeting!

(The following action takes place quickly and should not break the flow of the conversations, nor should it detract from the speaking actors. **SCOTT** *immediately enters from the theatre, running past* **HARRIET***. He goes to the rack and grabs a shawl.)*

DANIEL. You were wrapping a present...

VONDO. Bye, baby.
(hangs up)

MEREDITH. I can see it now. Opening night I'll be standing in the spotlight...

*(***ROBIN*** enters running from the trailer in a different dress. She stops for* **SCOTT** *to zip her dress, then he tosses the shawl over her shoulders as* **DANIEL** *says his line, "You were stirring a pot.")*

DANIEL. You were packing a bag?

(JEANNIE,
*defeated, sits
on the back of
the van, next
to* **MIKE***)*

MEREDITH. and Kurt
will be playing
my Latin lover –
Menudo.

DANIEL. You were
stirring a pot…

SCOTT. *(to* **ROBIN***)*
Go, go, go!

*(***ROBIN** *and* **SCOTT** *exit, running into the theatre, passing* **HARRIET**. *She follows closing the door.)*

MEREDITH. And
then my
mariachi band
will begin to
play. *(she points
to* **VONDO***)*

*(***VONDO** *plays* Smoke on the Water.*)*[*]

DANIEL. You were
making a bed…

---

[*] See Music Use Note on Page 3.

MEREDITH. and Kurt will serenade me with a beautiful Mexican ballad like… *(thinks hard)*

DANIEL. God, I know I can get this!

MEREDITH. like… *(Thinks harder. Sings counter to "Smoke on the Water")* Feliz Navi-dad…

(sings and by the van)

Feliz Navi-dad…

ERIC. *(to* **MIKE***)* How do you spell regurgitates?

*(***JEFF*** stands at the theatre door, gives a look back to* **MIKE***. Gives* **MIKE** *a small "farewell salute."* **MIKE** *gives* **JEFF** *an acknowledging nod and salute.* **JEFF** *smiles, EXITS into the theatre, closing the door.)*

MEREDITH. Feliz Navi-dad, la la la la la, la la la la la! *(continues singing)*

ERIC. *(proclaims front)* My God! WHAT A SEASON IT WILL BE!

DANIEL. *(Points to*
JEANNIE with a
big smile.) You
were sewing a
button! *(Smiling,*
he hits his
forehead with the
palm of his hand
as if he can't
believe he didn't
figure it out
sooner.) Duh!

(JEANNIE looks at MIKE *and lies back into the van with her feet dangling over the edge.* VONDO, *oblivious to everything, keeps playing. Lights dim to spot on* MIKE, *who looks at the keys, gives them a little toss, clenches them in his hand and smiles. Lights fade to black.)*

(curtain)

MANDATORY PLAYWRIGHT'S NOTES

Okay, you may read these notes and think, "Seriously—does she really have to tell us this?" Well recently I purchased a new curling iron and when removing the caution label I noticed one of the warnings read: "Do not use on eyelashes." I thought, "Seriously—do they really have to tell me this?" Then I realized, that warning was there because someone, somewhere, did it. That being said, I sincerely thank you for taking the time to read and follow these notes.

For those who may not be aware of this—all materials in this play are protected by copyright. This also includes protecting the artistic integrity of the work. By acquiring the rights to perform this play you are agreeing to adhere to the next three conditions as stated below:

1: Page 31; the exchange between Robin and Mike must be played as I wrote it. She does not realize the implications of what she is saying to Mike. She is merely repeating what Eric has told her. The whole "becoming a woman" stuff goes right over her head. It's everyone else who is listening that is unnerved by what she's saying—that's what makes it funny. The actor playing Robin cannot portray her sexy or as if she is coming on to Mike. It will make her look slutty and that is not the character. Her lines must be said innocently to Mike. For example: "I'm not wearing underwear," should be said as simply as if she was saying, "I got an A on my test today." Also, at no time can any of the male characters react to what she is saying as if it is affecting them sexually. Playing it that way will turn the moment creepy, it will look like you are going for a very, very cheap laugh and the audience will think I wrote it that way—which I didn't.

2: Page 57; what makes the exchange between Robin and Eric funny is that it sounds dirty—when it's not. The more oblivious Eric is to the double entendre dialogue, the funnier the scene will be. The actor playing Eric must never deliver any of this dialogue as if the character is aware of the sexual overtones. Also, he is not permitted to play the scene, or any other scene, like he is coming on to Robin. She is 15 and it will make the audience think he is a pervert, or worse, a pedophile. That will totally change the dynamic of the rest of the play, not only for his character, but for everyone and everything in future scenes. Also, Jeff and Mike would stop Eric immediately if they thought he was deliberately being inappropriate with Robin and if Eric was acting pervy, Robin would be afraid of him. Put these things together and not only have you just killed the comedy, you will not be able to recover it. I did not write this play to have any of these implications. Again, I cannot stress this strongly enough—no actor is permitted to play this scene, or any other scene, with sexual overtones or in a sexual nature.

3: You must perform the play as written and are not allowed do any of the following:
- •Change the gender of a character
- •Cut or double a character
- • Edit jokes, dialogue or scenes without the prior written permission of the author.

The comedy has been structured and something as simple adding, changing or reversing words can lessen a laugh or kill it completely. Please know I'm not just trying to protect my work, I'm trying to protect your production as well.

That's it for the mandatory stuff. Below are suggestions you can use if you want. They may help give you some ideas, especially with the van and exploding toga.

GENERAL SUGGESTIONS

The director should approach this play with an important element in mind—the clock is always ticking for these characters. Pace is key. The scenes take place right before curtain, at intermission or in the middle of a performance. There should always be an underlying sense of urgency for the characters. The plot should be continuously moving quickly with some places faster than others. Spots where you can slow it down a bit—Jeff telling Mike he's leaving (pg. 36), Harriet's Nantucket story (pg. 70), and the Mike and Meredith scene that follows (pg. 74).

This is not screwball comedy. Often it is thought that if a character is written funny, they should be played goofy, wacky or over the top. This doesn't mean you don't get big at times, just don't turn the play into a farce. In the final moments when the multiple conversations occur, everyone should be so sincerely excited and hopeful for the next season that the audience will truly like them all, divas included.

CHARACTER SUGGESTIONS

MIKE: He's a nice guy who has it together. He's got looks, talent, integrity and an unintentional charm that makes him likable from the start. He cares about doing good work. While he'll do all he can to avoid hurting someone, he's not a wimp. When a difficult situation arises, he is the first to defend and support those who need it. When handed a challenge, he'll take charge and work till he drops to see it through. But he does have his limits and if confronted, he will stand up for himself. This is the guy you want your daughter to date and your son to have as a best friend.

JEANNIE: She is more than happy to be in the background and will be the one to get the job done, no matter what it is. Most of her one-liners will provide the reality that some characters need to hear. The majority of her laugh lines are written for a dry delivery. The more matter of factly she says them, the funnier they are. Should a funny spin be put on her laugh lines, they don't go over as well. From experience I can say this has happened most every time. Dry is not dull however, so be careful of that. She can be sarcastic, but she is not mean. And no matter how much she pisses and moans, no matter how many actors drive her up a wall, were she given a choice, she wouldn't spend her summer anywhere else.

VONDO: He's a good soul with a good heart and a hard-partying druggie past. He's not stupid, just a little fried. Pick and choose where you might want to make him foggy. IMPORTANT: He is an older guy with a van, so be very careful not to make him look like he offers candy to children. He should not be scary or look like a bum. He is not violent but when pushed past his limit, he can lose it big time and pounce. He is very proud of the theatre and his work there. He's goes with the flow, is a team player and genuinely likes everyone—as long as they don't touch his cooler.

MEREDITH: She so desperately wants to be someone and when not at the theatre, she knows she fades into the background. She's more neurotic than nasty. Angst will work better than anger; pick and choose when she yells. If she is screaming and nasty from start to finish, she'll give the audience a headache, they won't understand what Mike sees in her and most important, they'll have no empathy for her in the Glass Menagerie scene. That moment with Mike is her moment to show her heart. If she plays that scene right, the audience will not only develop a little soft spot for her, by the show's last few moments, they might almost be rooting for her as well.

ERIC: He is not an evil villain- avoid playing him that way. He's a pompous, self-important jerk who truly wants his crap to be seen as art. He sucks as a playwright, he sucks as a director, but he doesn't suck as an actor—and everyone there knows it. He can be odd, but do not make him creepy. His arrogance (which he uses as a defense mechanism) stems from a lack of confidence and he does not make friends easily. But that's not because he thinks people don't like him, he thinks they just don't understand him. While he may be a loser whose intentions for the playhouse are questionable, he really does love it there and just wants someone, one time, to think he's done something good.

DANIEL: Daniel lives in his Daniel bubble. He always thinks it's about him, even when it's not. He's totally unaware he's kind of a moron and has no clue how much he grates on people's nerves. He will only see his side of the story. No matter how hard you try to explain something, if it's not what he wants to hear, he won't get it. Nobody is sure if he's gay or straight and the actor playing him should be aware of this when developing the character. He is annoying, but should be a fun annoying—so much so that audience should actually look forward to getting annoyed by him. This is one of the most difficult characters to play. He has to be big at times, but if you go too over the top, he can become a cartoon. If he's too bratty, he's not likable and if he's too obnoxious, he can become unbearable. The actor and director must walk a thin line with him. But as long as you can make all his needy dopiness fun, the audience will love him.

JEFF: Does not suffer fools lightly. When he loses his temper it's due to him being totally frustrated, stressed and annoyed. Anyone who's ever encountered the administrative side of theatre knows this feeling well. Watch that you don't make his threats sound too vicious because while he can be intimidating, the audience still has to like him. Though he won't show it, he realizes if the theatre closes many of the people there (including the ones he wants to smack) could lose the only thing in their lives that really brings them happiness. This really gets to him. He trusts his instincts to hand the theatre over to Mike, but has a really tough time letting go of the control.

HARRIET: She is a genuine, well-spoken, accomplished woman who knows who she is. Avoid at all costs making her the "sassy old lady." Many of her lines are zingers, but they should never come across as bitter or nasty. She will speak her mind if need be, but she always does it with class— even if she's saying something a little bit racy. Unlike some people there, when she leaves the theatre she still has a life— and a good one at that.

SCOTT: He is the character that takes one of the biggest journeys. He starts off as the awkward outsider, but with every scene he grows a little more comfortable with his position, the people around him and himself. By the end, not only is he one of the company, he has found a home. Important: He is a nice guy who happens to be gay. Do not make him flaming or a stereotype. This does not mean he can't have a moment or two of fabulousness—but it should be an endearing fabulousness, not a Liberace fabulousness.

ROBIN: She is truly a sweet breath of fresh air that everyone (sans Meredith) sincerely loves. When she hugs someone, she means it. She works hard and really tries to do the best she can. She will get upset if something goes wrong, but she is not whiny. Being young and growing up a bit sheltered, she is way too trusting and totally naïve. But this makes her innocent, not stupid. Avoid playing her dumb.

THE VAN

The van should be as far downstage as you can allow since a great deal of action revolves around it. It should have two doors that open from the center, not one door that lifts up like an SUV. Two door van allows the actors to been seen better, plus it is SO much easier to light. Suggestions for dressing the van— this is Vondo's home away from home and stuff hanging/taped inside the van should reflect that. Some stuff can be recent, but other stuff should be aged to look as though it's been hanging there for years. Past productions included: a John Belushi poster from Animal House, a picture of Farrah Faucet, some covers from Rolling Stone, Creem and/or Mad magazines, old album covers: Pink Floyd, Allman Brothers, Clapton, (you can also use Jethro Tull, Lynyrd Skynyrd, Zappa or the obvious, Grateful Dead), show posters, some old photos- his parents, his prom picture, one of his cat, you get the idea. Do not use anything dirty or creepy. No Playboy, porn or horror movie posters. Any bumper stickers should be aged so they don't look like they were put on yesterday. A favorite that was used, "Rehab is for Quitters". There are three ways you can go with the van:

Option 1: If your facility can manage it and your stage is strong enough, drive or push a full size van on stage. At a past festival production, they used a real van and opted to drive it onstage. In order to do this they were required to sign a paper for the local fire department stating the gas tank would contain no more than a gallon of gas. This was for fire safety purposes. Should you use a real van, you might want to keep that in mind.

Option 2: Get what's called a "clip" of a van. Go to your local chop shop or car demolition lot and ask them to cut off the front part of the van. That will give you approximately 5 feet of the back half of a van. The biggest hurdles are getting it to the theatre and getting it onstage. You will need a decent size crew, as it will be extremely heavy. You will need to build a strong support to hold up the front half as well as a small platform so the van doesn't end exactly at the point where the clip was cut. It should extend about 3 feet past the curtain separating the back of the van from the front. That is so an actor can "go to the front of the van" if needed. The missing front of the van will probably need to be masked from the audience. A fence or some trees will help. There should be a curtain that separates the front of the van from the back, masking the need for a windshield, steering wheel, etc, and giving the illusion it's a full size van. Using the clip is very effective. It's not cheap, but it's not horribly costly either. Sometimes you can talk the chop shop into donating it.

Option 3: Build the van. Again, go to a chop shop or auto demolition lot and get two van doors (preferably with windows), a rear bumper, a license plate and tires. You can get taillights, or you may be able to use red reflectors that can be purchased at a home improvement store. Then you will then have to build the cab of the van. The corners of the cab should be rounded. You'll find plenty of photos online and it shouldn't be too hard to build it to scale. Use 2 or 4 tires, to hide the legs of the support or cut a tire in half and using a half on each side. You can use mud flaps, which helps to mask the tires if needed. As before, be careful how the van is placed onstage so that the missing front is masked from the audience. Again there should be a curtain that separates the back from the front. If you don't build a full cab, the platform should extend about 3 feet or more past the van curtain. You'll need to strongly secure the van doors to the cab. The doors are never used and are always left opened, which allows you to secure them well.

THE EXPLODING TOGA

If you come up with a better idea for Robin's toga in Medea, by all means go for it. There have been variations on this but here is the design that efficiently worked for us. Be aware— it's risky and you must be extremely careful when doing it this way. But done correctly, it works great every time. Here is what you will need:

- A white flannel backed vinyl tablecloth
- White mesh fabric or a good size white mesh laundry bag to be cut into pieces
- Laces, or something of that nature, to tie the blood jacket in the back
- A box of fold top (not zip-lock) sandwich bags
- A funnel
- Stage blood
- The toga costume, which goes over the blood packet jacket. The toga should be all white with maybe a little design or trim around the neck and floor length. It should be designed so the actor can easily walk into it.
- Backup blood jacket and toga. It's just a good idea.

For the blood jacket make the tablecloth into a version of a sleeveless hospital gown. The tablecloth works well because the blood will stay on top of the vinyl, letting it soak into the upper toga. That helps the blood to spread over the outer garment. Plus it helps keep the blood off the actor.

The blood jacket should have an open back so the actor can easily walk into it. It should tie easily in the back at the top and middle of the jacket. It should not be too tight or too baggy and end just below the crotch.

Cut the mesh fabric in teardrop shapes, approximately 4 inches at the base of the teardrop, tapering up to about a 1 inch opening at the top. The shape should be around 3 inches high.

On the front of the garment, place the mesh teardrops, with the widest part of the teardrop, right where the actor's nipples are. (Sorry- no delicate way to say that.) If there's room, try another teardrop in between the breasts so there are 3 across. (You may not be able to get away with that one.) Place another 3 teardrops at the top of her stomach. If you can safely fit more, try, but do not put any on the back. I suggest safety pinning the teardrops on the garment first. That way, after you've tested the jacket and run the popping hug a couple of times, you'll know the best areas to place the blood bags and you can sew the teardrops on.

Take the plastic sandwich bags and put one into each teardrop, pushing it down through the 1inch opening at the top into the bottom part of the teardrop. You need to have at least a half-inch of plastic overlap at the top part of each teardrop.

Take the funnel and CAREFULLY pour the blood in the plastic bags. Make sure the bottom part is very full but DO NOT POUR THE BLOOD ALL THE WAY TO THE TOP. It's easier to fill the teardrops at the top first. Make sure there's no spillage or it will seep through the outer toga too soon.

Loading the blood must be done pre-show. Hang it carefully and in a spot where no one will touch or bump into it. Seriously, treat it like a live grenade with a loose pin.

Right before her entrance, carefully put the actor in the blood jacket and tie it in the back. Carefully put the toga on her. She should not be in it for a long duration of time before her entrance. Also, the actor should move as little as possible when she is offstage and needs to be extremely careful when she onstage. Other actors should keep their distance from her until after she pops. Having the blood bags open is risky but it assures the blood will gush when she hugs Vondo. Sealed blood packets were used once, but didn't always pop efficiently. If done correctly, she will gush all over the place. It didn't fail us once.

Blood recipe: Trial and error with the measurements. We used one part Karo syrup, one part Deft detergent mixed with red, blue and yellow food coloring. Using detergent in the mix makes it easy to wash and prevents the blood from staining the toga. You'll have to play with the blood color pending the brand of food coloring you use. The color may not blend well if you use a blue detergent like Tide. We were able to wash the vinyl blood jacket too, but did not put it in the dryer. Check the tablecloth's washing instructions beforehand.

COSTUME AND PROP SUGGESTIONS

The costumes in general shouldn't look "professional". The show is set at a community theatre and should reflect that. But they should not look crappy or ridiculously over the top either. You may want some characters to under dress their costumes for quick changes, so plan ahead. Scene and costume changes should run quickly and no more than 30-45 seconds tops.

Here is a costume plot and a very basic prop list from a previous production you can use as a guide if you'd like:

ACT I
SCENE I: HELLO DOLLY

MIKE: Khaki pants, tee shirt, polo shirt or casual buttoned down shirt (whichever is easiest to get off the fastest), top sides (or a shoe that can be removed quickly)

JEANNIE: "Tech blacks." Black pants, black tee shirt

VONDO: Jeans, an aged band tee shirt

JEFF: Pants, button down shirt, possible tie

HARRIET (as Dolly Ensemble): Long skirt, lacy blouse, hat and parasol

MEREDITH (as Dolly): Red Dolly dress, feathers in hair, glitzy diamond necklace

ERIC: Solid black pants, black turtle neck, black boots if possible

DANIEL (as Waiter): Black pants, white shirt, black bow tie, red vest, black shoes.

ROBIN (as Minnie Fay): Ruffled long skirt, lacy blouse, big bow in hair

SCOTT: Pressed khaki pants, a pressed buttoned up short sleeve shirt, topsiders

SCENE II: SOUND OF MUSIC

MIKE (as Rolf): NOTE: No swastika, very tight and short khaki or military color Nazi youth shorts, khaki or military shirt, possible suspenders, knee socks, work boots or shoes with a buckle, military delivery boy cap

JEANNIE: shorts and a show tee shirt (should not be brightly colored)

VONDO: Jeans, print button down shirt (maybe Hawaiian) worn over previous tee shirt, baseball cap backwards

ERIC: Black pants, Clockwork Orange, Eraserhead or Reservoir Dogs tee shirt

JEFF: Summer pants, short sleeve button down shirt

ROBIN: Oversized shirt with shorts and tee shirt. Second Change: (as Liesl) White sailor blouse with navy blue trim, white pleated skirt, Note: must be white ankle socks. No tights (it will ruin the "no underwear" joke)

SCOTT: Jeans, tee shirt, pressed buttoned short sleeve shirt worn open over tee.

DANIEL (as Captain von Trapp): Austrian jacket, white shirt, pants
MEREDITH (as Maria von Trapp): Novice habit with wimple
HARRIET (Mother Abbess): Full Mother Superior habit

SCENE III: MEDEA

JEANNIE: Shorts, different tee shirt
VONDO: Jeans, light colored tee shirt. Note: the shirt can have a logo
   on the back or a small on a breast pocket on the front.
MIKE: Jeans, tee shirt
SCOTT: khaki shorts, un-tucked polo shirt, sneakers
ROBIN (as Medea's daughter): Pink toga, with pink flowers in hair,
   Second Change: blood packet jacket, white toga, flower laurel on
   head.
DANIEL (as Medea's husband): Toga, laurel around head, sandals
ERIC: Black pants, black dress shirt with bolo tie
MEREDITH (as Medea): Toga, big Grecian jewelry, sandals
JEFF: Summer pants with short sleeve button down shirt
HARRIET: Summer skirt, blouse or summer pants suit

ACT II
SCENE I: OKLAHOMA

JEANNIE (as Women's Ensemble): 1906 gingham party dress, lace up
   work boots, hick hat with sunflower
SCOTT: shorts, un-tucked tee shirt, tape measure around his neck,
   sneakers.
VONDO (as Back end of a Cow): Willy Wonka or Oompa Loopma tee
   shirt (Gene Wilder version), tee shirt must be aged, cow pants (can
   be white medical scrubs with black felt cow spots sewn on), bandan-
   na made of cow fabric worn on head
MIKE: Khaki pants, button down short sleeve shirt
ERIC (as Jud Fry): Dark brown pants or jeans, dark color country western shirt, leather or suede vest, dark work boots
JEFF: Summer pants, button down short sleeve shirt
DANIEL (as Will Parker): Cowboy pants, suede chaps (optional) country western shirt, cowboy boots, cowboy hat, neckerchief
MEREDITH (as Ado Annie): 1906 country girl dress, cute little hat.
ROBIN (as Laurey): 1906 farm girl skirt, country looking blouse, bow
   in hair.
HARRIET (as Aunt Eller): 1906 long skirt, apron, country looking
   blouse, shawl

SCENE II: GLASS MENAGIRE

JEFF: pants, tee shirt, short sleeve shirt worn open
MEREDITH: Summer dress, or pants/Capri's with summer shirt
JEANNIE: Shorts, tee shirt
VONDO: Jeans or shorts, tee shirt

MIKE: Summer pants with button down shirt, possible tie

ROBIN (as Laura): 1940's drab dress with bow in hair

DANIEL: Black shorts, black socks, black shoes, a black tee shirt with, Mime the Musical written on the front and a big face of a mime on the back

HARRIET (as Amanda): 1940's drab dress.

ERIC (as Tom): Pants, shirt, pee-coat, plain black stocking hat, black shoes

SCOTT: Loose fitting, knee length gym shorts, show tee shirt untucked

SCENE III: WEST SIDE STORY

JEANNIE, shorts, tee shirt

SCOTT: Wrinkled cargo shorts, wrinkled button down shirt worn open over a Joan Crawford tee shirt.

VONDO: (as Glad Hand) Early 1960-ish jacket, black or brown pants, shirt, bow tie horn-rim glasses, porkpie hat (optional), SECOND CHANGE: (as King) Tunic or robe, cape (if time allows), crown, scepter, THIRD CHANGE: (as Vondo) Remove tunic/robe, cape, crown, leaving him in pants and a tee shirt.

MIKE: Khaki pants, dress shirt—can be short sleeve, tie

JEFF: Summer pants, Hawaiian or tropical print shirt

HARRIET: Summer pants outfit

ROBIN: (as Maria): White dress, red belt, red shoes, bow in hair, SECOND CHANGE: (as Maria) Pastel color dressed, matching bow in hair

MEREDITH: (as Anita) 1960's Mambo dress, SECOND CHANGE: (as Anita) Spanish looking skirt, peasant blouse, shawl

ERIC (as Bernardo): Purple or white tee shirt, black pants

DANIEL (as Tony): Button down short sleeve shirt, pants

PROPERTIES LIST

Act I   Scene I

PRESET	marquee (Hello Dolly)
PRESET	costume rack with tarp
PRESET	cooler
VONDO	guitar & amp
HARRIET	beer (Rheingold)
MIKE	church window frame
MIKE	colored construction paper with scissors
JEANNIE	tape
ROBIN	Playbill
SCOTT	clipboard (pencil attached with string)
VONDO	cell phone
SCOTT	women's evening gloves
JEFF	red gels
VONDO	something small to fix (power strip, light, prop)
VONDO	screwdriver

Act I   Scene II

PRESET	marquee (The Sound of Music)
PRESET	costume rack w/different costumes (tarp optional)
VONDO	cell phone
JEANNIE	box marked "Medea"
JEANNIE	list of body parts
ERIC	stocking shaped like long intestine
ERIC	Cliff Notes
JEANNIE	clay (inside Medea box) pink Play-Doh
JEANNIE	short hose (inside Medea box)
MIKE	script (Sound of Music) with pocket containing cd
MIKE	cd
VONDO	guitar & amp
JEFF	script (Sound of Music)

Act I   Scene III

PRESET	marquee (Medea)
PRESET	costume rack w/different costumes (tarp optional)

VONDO	cooler
VONDO	cell phone
ERIC	bloody leg
JEANNIE	staple gun
VONDO	teddy bear with laurel on head
MIKE	laundry-type bag containing rags
JEANNIE	roll of paper towels
SCOTT	large garbage bag w/hole cut at bottom
MEREDITH	severed head
MIKE	prop box (labeled Blood & Guts)
ERIC	Backpack w/Cliff's Notes, notebooks, ice cream scoop
ERIC/MIKE	Garbage to throw from van – Yoohoo can, papers, gels, cereal boxes, scripts, clothes, etc.
VONDO	guitar & amp
JEFF	Tums

Act II Scene I

PRESET	marquee (Oklahoma)
PRESET	costume rack w/different costumes (tarp optional)
JEANNIE	pickle barrel
MIKE	clipboard with pencil, mail and papers
SCOTT	ornate crown
JEANNIE	basket (Oklahoma picnic)
MIKE	cooler
ROBIN	basket (Oklahoma picnic)
MEREDITH	basket (Oklahoma picnic)
JEFF	keys
VONDO	Yoo-hoo

Act II Scene II

PRESET	marquee (Glass Menagerie)
VONDO	Yoo-hoo (2)
VONDO	Cheetos
MEREDITH	cell phone
JEANNIE	dress (from rack)
MIKE	Sheaf of paperwork

Act II Scene III

PRESET	marquee (West Side Story)
PRESET	costume rack w/half West Side Story costumes and half Sleeping Beauty costumes
PRESET	cooler
HARRIET	costume
HARRIET	needle & thread
JEANNIE	Tunic/robe
JEANNIE	Crown
JEANNIE	scepter
VONDO	cell phone
VONDO	Yoo-hoo
DANIEL	list of plays
MEREDITH	Smartphone or iPad to look at pictures
JEANNIE	small note pad
VONDO	guitar & amp
JEFF	keys
ERIC	backpack
ERIC	notebook

SAMUEL FRENCH STAFF

Nate Collins
President

Ken Dingledine
Director of Operations,
Vice President

Bruce Lazarus
Executive Director,
General Counsel

Rita Maté
Director of Finance

ACCOUNTING

Lori Thimsen | Director of Licensing Compliance
Nehal Kumar | Senior Accounting Associate
Glenn Halcomb | Royalty Administration
Jessica Zheng | Accounts Receivable
Andy Lian | Accounts Payable
Charlie Sou | Accounting Associate
Joann Mannello | Orders Administrator

BUSINESS AFFAIRS

Caitlin Bartow | Assistant to the Executive Director

CORPORATE COMMUNICATIONS

Abbie Van Nostrand | Director of Corporate
Communications

CUSTOMER SERVICE AND LICENSING

Brad Lohrenz | Director of Licensing Development
Laura Lindson | Licensing Services Manager
Kim Rogers | Theatrical Specialist
Matthew Akers | Theatrical Specialist
Ashley Byrne | Theatrical Specialist
Jennifer Carter | Theatrical Specialist
Annette Storckman | Theatrical Specialist
Dyan Flores | Theatrical Specialist
Sarah Weber | Theatrical Specialist
Nicholas Dawson | Theatrical Specialist
David Kimple | Theatrical Specialist

EDITORIAL

Amy Rose Marsh | Literary Manager
Ben Coleman | Literary Associate

MARKETING

Ryan Pointer | Marketing Manager
Courtney Kochuba | Marketing Associate
Chris Kam | Marketing Associate

PUBLICATIONS AND PRODUCT DEVELOPMENT

Joe Ferreira | Product Development Manager
David Geer | Publications Manager
Charlyn Brea | Publications Associate
Tyler Mullen | Publications Associate
Derek P. Hassler | Musical Products Coordinator
Zachary Orts | Musical Materials Coordinator

OPERATIONS

Casey McLain | Operations Supervisor
Elizabeth Minski | Office Coordinator, Reception
Coryn Carson | Office Coordinator, Reception

SAMUEL FRENCH BOOKSHOP (LOS ANGELES)

Joyce Mehess | Bookstore Manager
Cory DeLair | Bookstore Buyer
Sonya Wallace | Bookstore Associate
Tim Coultas | Bookstore Associate
Alfred Contreras | Shipping & Receiving

LONDON OFFICE

Anne-Marie Ashman | Accounts Assistant
Felicity Barks | Rights & Contracts Associate
Steve Blacker | Bookshop Associate
David Bray | Customer Services Associate
Robert Cooke | Assistant Buyer
Stephanie Dawson | Amateur Licensing Associate
Simon Ellison | Retail Sales Manager
Robert Hamilton | Amateur Licensing Associate
Peter Langdon | Marketing Manager
Louise Mappley | Amateur Licensing Associate
James Nicolau | Despatch Associate
Martin Phillips | Librarian
Panos Panayi | Company Accountant
Zubayed Rahman | Despatch Associate
Steve Sanderson | Royalty Administration Supervisor
Douglas Schatz | Acting Executive Director
Roger Sheppard | I.T. Manager
Debbie Simmons | Licensing Sales Team Leader
Peter Smith | Amateur Licensing Associate
Garry Spratley | Customer Service Manager
David Webster | UK Operations Director
Sarah Wolf | Rights Director

GET THE NAME OF YOUR CAST AND CREW IN PRINT WITH SPECIAL EDITIONS!

Special Editions are a unique, fun way to commemorate your production and RAISE MONEY.

The Samuel French Special Edition is a customized script personalized to *your* production. Your cast and crew list, photos from your production and special thanks will all appear in a Samuel French Acting Edition alongside the original text of the play.

These Special Editions are powerful fundraising tools that can be sold in your lobby or throughout your community in advance.

These books have autograph pages that make them perfect for year book memories, or gifts for relatives unable to attend the show. Family and friends will cherish this one of a kind souvenier.

Everyone will want a copy of these beautiful, personalized scripts!

ORDER YOUR COPIES TODAY!
E-MAIL SPECIALEDITIONS@SAMUELFRENCH.COM
OR CALL US AT 1-866-598-8449!